LA
133.1
WOR
Word, Christine.
Ghosts along the Bayou : tales of hauntings in Southwestern Louisiana

90746017

DISCARD

Caldwell Parish Library
Ghosts along the Bayou : tales of hauntings in ...
Word, Christine.

9074 6017

 CALDWELL PARISH LIBRARY
P.O. BOX 1499
COLUMBIA, LA 71418

GHOSTS ALONG THE BAYOU

GHOSTS ALONG THE BAYOU

TALES OF HAUNTINGS IN SOUTHWESTERN LOUISIANA

CHRISTINE WORD

DISCARDWORD press

Lafayette, Louisiana
1997

Copyright 1988 by Christine Word. All rights reserved.

International Standard Book Number: 0-9661585-0-4

Library of Congress Catalog Card Number: 88-72354

WORD
press

106 Brigante Place
Lafayette, La. 70508
1997

Printed in the United States of America

To my Duke,
who,
even when he
didn't believe in ghosts,
believed in me.

CONTENTS

Preface ix

STORIES
1. Marland's Bridge, Sunset 1
2. Eyes of the Pirates, Grand Marais 8
3. Home to Stay, Lafayette 18
4. The Spirit of Butcher Switch, Lafayette 25
5. The House of History, Washington 28
6. The Girl in the Attic, Washington 33
7. The Dreamies, St. Martinville 36
8. Addie at Susie, Centerville 42
9. The Spanish Trail Spectre, Crowley 47
10. Prissy and Pussy, New Iberia 52
11. The Gardening Ghost, Lafayette 56
12. Mysteries at Jefferson Island 59
13. The Phantom of Poiret Place, Plaissance ... 69
14. An August Aura, New Iberia 71
15. Yankee Headquarters Still? Sunset 75
16. Marshmallow, Grand Coteau 87
17. Night Caller, Broussard 93
18. Sarah's Curse, Iberia Parish 97
19. 'T Frere's Amelie, Lafayette 102
20. Shoes on the Stairs, Franklin 111
21. The Ghost of Grand Prairie, St. Landry ... 115
22. Glenda's Ghost, New Iberia 124
23. Strangers in the Night, Broussard 127
24. Time Traveler, Vermilion Parish 132
25. The Haunted Rectory, Abbeville 135

Epilogue 141
Index 145

PREFACE

This book is not an attempt to prove or disprove the existence of ghosts and haunted places. Rather it is an unembellished account of strange occurrences as told to me by people kind enough to trust me with their tales.

It is also an indulgenge in my fascination with the unknown. Though I have long been interested in the subject of ghosts, I never seriously considered an avocation as a ghosthunter, at least not until my curiousity was aroused in the unlikely setting of an economics classroom. My professor, Dr. David C. Edmonds, happened to be writing a narrative of the Civil War in this area when I took the course, and he occasionally regaled the class with stories he had come across in his research, including a few that occurred in his own house.

Ten years later when I decided to write this book, I renewed my acquaintance with Dr. Edmonds to inquire if I could use his story. His reply was that not only could I use his story (see "Yankee Headquarters Still?"), but that he had collected leads to other stories, mostly through his students, in hopes of someday writing such a book himself. Since he had decided to forego the project, he said I was welcome to these files!

So began my search for ghosts along the bayou.

My research has consisted almost entirely of personal interviews with people who have had first-hand encounters. Whenever I heard of such experiences, no matter how trivial, I telephoned the occupants to arrange an interview, preferably at the location of the disturbance. During these interviews, I used both a tape recorder and notes. Only once was I asked not to use my recorder. One story usually led to another. Occasionally someone would ask that I not reveal their identity. In these instances—which I have so noted—I have substituted pseudonyms, or simply refer to them by other means. All other names are real.

I owe my sincere appreciation to my pastor, Father Robie Robichaux, for sharing his thoughts with me on this subject in the epilogue. I am also indebted to many other people, not the least of whom is my sister, Helaine Dunbar, who not only keyed my stories into her computer, but also worked out numerous problems of a technical nature, some of them so perplexing that she began to wonder about this ghost business. I truly appreciate Helaine's time, patience, persistence and humor.

Since I have five children, babysitters had to be my first consideration in scheduling appointments. I am indebted to Sue and Pam Milsaps, my dependable neighbors, and to my dear Mother, Margarette Kennedy, whom I relied on immensely. The freedom they gave me to pursue this project is a wonderful treasure.

And Connie Gatlin, whose recent acquaintance I am happy to have made. Connie has had many years of experience as a freelance writer, and she graciously volunteered her special gift of insight, support, generosity of time and expertise, and many helpful suggestions.

Many other wonderful, interesting people provided stories, and are noted in the main text (except for those who wish to remain anonymous); others provided valuable leads to other stories, among them Michelle Edelbrock, Betty Soileau, Robley Domingue, Evelyn Landry, June Pitre, Rosie Scammel, Simone Guillory, Margarette Kennedy, Gail Hebert, Lucinda Edmonds, Karen Bernard, Mrs. Clarence Leger and a few others whom I did not meet. But I am no less grateful.

Thanks also to Jeff Fuchs, the talented artist who illustrated the book, to "Cat" Landry, who assisted with the dust jacket, to Tammy Labiche, who donated her computer skills in preparing the manuscript, and to members of the Writer's Guild of Acadiana for their friendship, motivation and advice.

In particular, I express appreciation to my father, Sam Kennedy, and my brother, Sam Kennedy, Jr.; also to Suzanne Tierney who helped launch my writing career, to Mary Alice Fontenot, Ron and Wanda Bourque, Trent Angers, Maxine Duhon, Kathy Lowry, Darrel Landry, Kirby Bertrand and my confidants, Mary Blair and my sister, Lois Melancon.

I wish especially to give my heartfelt thanks to Dr. David C. Edmonds, my teacher, editor, and friend. His initial enthusiasm, continual encouragement and writing expertise turned an idea into an accomplishment for a ghosthunter who really wanted to be an author.

Christine Word
Broussard, Louisiana

MARLAND'S BRIDGE

If violent death can cause a spirit to linger near the scene of its earthly demise, then battlefields and murder sites must surely be among the most haunted of places. And, indeed, there's a bridge in St. Landry Parish, near the town of Sunset, which qualifies on both accounts.

It's appearance is simple but intriguing: a rickety wooden structure with wide planks and railing. A winding little bayou with coffee-colored water and dark, sloping banks. Some overhanging limbs and the darkness of thick, surrounding woods.

The bridge has a fascinating history. For one thing, it's the site of the Battle of Bayou Bourbeux, where Confederate Texans routed and captured an entire Union brigade in one of the bloodiest Civil War clashes in Louisiana. The Texans who died on that bloody November morning in 1863 are still buried nearby. So are a large number of runaway slaves and a few Yankees.

Yet the site has gone unmarked and forgotten,

and until very recently was little more than a convenient dumping site for discarded washing machines, refrigerators, other garbage – and a few bodies.

With such a background as this, it's no wonder that the bridge has long been surrounded by unearthly events.

Just ask Russell Montgomery, who lives up the road toward Opelousas. "There's something mysterious about that bridge," he says, remembering his own encounters in this otherwise quiet, rural residential area. He's seen a woman there two or three times at night.

So has Paul Oppenheimer, a medical professional who occasionally hunts for relics in the area. Paul's first encounter with the strange lady on the bridge was late last summer, just at dusk, while he was driving through: "I knew it wasn't a person because it was like floating off the ground. It was a woman because it had on a white dress."

Paul, speaking to me in the study of his home near Lafayette, says that when he came to within about a hundred yards of the apparition, he stopped the car, looked, and saw it was still there: "But when I got close, it disappeared. I didn't see a face; it was more like a skull: big, dark, sunken eyes. She didn't have any feet. I wasn't frightened of her, but when I got close and it disappeared, I got frightened...then I knew it was that girl that they killed."

Paul is referring to a body that was found about fifteen years ago in the woods near the bridge. The girl—apparently in her late teens—had been brutally raped and murdered. Her killer was never found.

Kathy and David Sturgis, an attractive young

couple who lives on the east side of the bridge, just a few houses away, have had even more startling experiences. So startling, in fact—and out of the ordinary—that they were at first hesitant to talk about it, even to one another. And as I speak with them in Kathy's office, each seems relieved to hear that I have uncovered similar stories from other people.

David, an oil company executive with an interest in coaching (and a side line in taxidermy) tells me that his first encounter with the lady occurred not long ago. It was just after dark, and he was in his car on his way to a nearby store: "As I approached the bridge, I saw a woman standing there. She was a light gray figure, and turned toward the water like she was looking at it. As I got real close...it just disappeared across the road. Kind of like smoke; like a vacuum cleaner sucked something across the road. When that happened my car radio switched from FM to AM, and I had the eeriest feeling."

David was so rattled by the experience that he forgot what he needed at the store. Returning home, he told Kathy only that he'd seen something at the bridge that gave him a funny feeling.

A few days later, Kathy had her own encounter. It was late afternoon, with plenty of daylight left. Kathy had just returned home from her job as a sales consultant for a large motel chain and decided to take a walk with the children. The family dog, Goldie, went with them. Along the way, the kids stopped off for a couple of minutes at a neighbor's house; Kathy and Goldie continued on, walking straight toward the bridge. Momentarily, the dog started acting up, holding her head back and whimpering while gazing toward the bridge.

Then Kathy looked: "There was a woman standing on the bridge. Since she had on a coat and I was in shorts, I wondered, 'Who is that?' She was just standing there in this beige, London Fog-looking coat staring at me. I couldn't see the face...it was a smear."

Considering the circumstances, Kathy was remarkably observant, noticing the long brown hair, the fact that it was stringy, and seemed to be blowing in the breeze: "She looked like a young person. I don't remember seeing her hands and feet. I kept looking at her, and then I turned to see where the kids were. When I looked back, she was still there, just staring at me."

Kathy had not previously heard of the mysterious lady of the bridge, so she kept on walking toward her, wondering who she was and what she was doing there...and in that coat on such a warm day. By this time, the kids had caught up, and were riding their bikes close behind: "The lady wasn't moving, but when we got about ten feet closer, her whole body lifted up and, kind of like you throw a napkin, it just drifted as if it had no bones in it [Kathy uses her arm to describe an undulating motion] and went under the bridge...."

Kathy, almost frantic now, called the kids. By the tone of her voice they knew something was wrong and came rushing up immediately. "What's wrong, Mom?" they asked.

"There's something under that bridge," she answered. "We're not going across."

Kathy says she thinks of the chilling sight every time she goes across the old bridge, which is as little as possible.

Larry Leger, an auto broker in Grand Coteau, has also seen the mysterious lady. He owns a picturesque camp adjacent to the bridge, on land recently cleared of heavy underbrush and the castoffs that had accumulated there over the years. There is a clear view of the bridge from his front yard, and he's seen her twice, both times at night. On both occasions she seemed to be wearing a veil, and she floated—rather than stood—on the bridge.

"When I talk about it," he says, sitting in his office in Grand Coteau, "it gives me an eerie feeling." Larry glances toward his elbow and says, "Look at the hair on my arms!"

Larry tells me about the time he was traveling over the bridge in his car when the figure of a woman suddenly appeared in his headlights. Startled, he slammed on the brakes: "She was staring right at me, and that's what gets to me."

He feels certain that many other people have also seen the lady on the bridge, including people who visit his camp, but don't want to admit it. And he's noticed the strange behavior of animals, mainly dogs and horses that won't cross the bridge, or which act up as they approach it. "But," says Larry, smiling, "I can't cross the bridge myself without getting the chills."

Unlike Paul, who ties the apparition to a murder, Larry thinks that it has to do with the Civil War battle. In this connection he draws my attention to a bookcase, and shows me a rusty projectile which was found near his camp on the banks of the Bayou Bourbeux. Larry explains that it is a Schenkle shell, that it is still live, and that it probably came from a Massachusetts artillery battery that was known to have used this sort of weapon.

And, indeed, I later find an account of the battle in *Yankee Autumn in Acadiana*, by David Edmonds. According to Edmonds, there was a twenty-three-year-old gunnery lieutenant named William Marland, 2nd Massachusetts Battery of Light Artillery (Nims' Battery), who succeeded in rushing the bayou with his eight-horse team and large artillery piece although the bridge was in the hands of the 11th Texas Infantry.

Marland's lone charge across the bridge "caused several astonished Texans to jump or be dumped into the muddy waters." This heroic feat earned for him a Congressional Medal of Honor and much admiration, even to the temporary naming of this bridge "Marland's Bridge."

But Marland was one of the lucky few. Most of his brigade was captured that day; many others killed or wounded—along with large numbers of Confederate soldiers and runaway slaves. For many years afterwards the people who lived in the vicinity said they could still hear the sounds of battle: the shouts, the cries of wounded men and horses, sharp commands, and the rattle of musketry.

Although Russell Montgomery knows his Civil War history, he doesn't buy that explanation as the cause of the haunting. The bridge and the dark, surrounding woods, he points out, has been a dumping ground for bodies for years. This is well established in the police records of St. Landry Parish, which show that at least four, and possibly five, murder victims have been discovered there, all in the days before it grew into a quiet residential area.

Mr. Montgomery's description of what he saw

on the bridge ("a white veiled figure") is almost identical to that of Larry Leger. He also echoes the words of Kathy Sturgis when he says it looks like a "handkerchief floating as it drops." But none of the others have noticed the distinct musty odor which he says has characterized each of his sightings.

So the mystery remains: Is the lady on the bridge a victim of murder foul (and perhaps trying to tell us the identity of her murderer), or does she have something to do with the Civil War battle?

There's another possibility, and one that was communicated to me by telephone a few days after the publication of this story in a local newspaper. Many years ago, 1922 to be precise, a ten-year-old girl was killed there in a tragic accident. She was riding home on a school bus, a slow-moving, horse-drawn wagon. Seeing some wild flowers growing alongside the road, she hopped off the bus to gather some for her mother—and was immediately struck by an oncoming automobile driven by a school teacher.

So the mystery deepens. Could the apparition on the bridge be the spirit of the little girl, still searching for wild flowers? Or is it as Larry Leger suggests: that the lady is a guardian spirit watching over all the departed souls along Bayou Bourbeux?

Whatever the case, and whoever she may be, I keep thinking of Larry's words: "The lady's there...and if you pass there, you'll see her...at night."

EYES OF THE PIRATES

The moon was full that night, and the wind whistled through the cane as the young couple returning home rumbled down the dirt lane in their pick-up truck. As always, their eyes were drawn to the upstairs window. This time something moved. Something or someone. A light blue definite something. As they watched, the object moved to the side and out of view. They both saw that.

But when they searched the house, they found nothing.

Jackie Landry had become accustomed to the activity even though he thought things were finally settling down. But that was before he married Joyce six months earlier and brought her and her children to live in the house that he built.

Jackie and Joyce are down-to-earth working people who live in a country house in Iberia Parish. The house sits back off the road. The only approach is by a dirt lane through a cane field. I arrive there in the afternoon, and am soon seated around the dining table drinking coffee while Jackie and Joyce recount their experiences.

Jackie tells me that he first noticed noises when he lived in a mobile home on the same site. It became worse after he built his home there.

Every morning before sunrise there's the sound of a door slamming. "Sounds like a trunk closing," Joyce says. The slamming occurs at other times of the day, and sometimes at night. She says visitors are often perplexed when no one arrives after they hear the noise.

Even when Jackie was building this rustic,

two-story house—he's a carpenter by profession—he felt there was something watching him. And then one morning about two years ago he woke up to find he was not alone: "I saw five pirates standing around this table," he says. It was just before sunrise and he had been sleeping on the daybed in the living room adjoining the dining area. Since he lived alone then, he slept with a .357 Magnum at his side. He immediately drew it and sat up to face the intruders.

But they quickly disappeared.

The next morning he woke up to find the same five pirate-looking characters standing around again, all of them colorfully dressed, some with bandannas around their heads. They seemed to be watching him. He drew his gun slowly this time, and again they vanished.

On the third morning he sensed their presence even before he opened his eyes. This time he decided against pulling his gun, and instead slowly sat up at the side of his bed for a good look. Though their clothing was colorful, they appeared dirty and were somewhat scraggly-looking, partly because of their long unkempt hair and beards. They seemed to be talking amongst themselves, but without any sounds of voices. After a while they looked over at him as though they sensed his intrusion on their conversation. Jackie, feeling bold, said, "I want to talk to y'all."

Again they vanished, but this time it was a slow fading-out instead of a sudden disappearance. Jackie says he hasn't seen them since.

Still, their presence seems to remain, and Jackie occasionally gets "these cold chills like something was here." He says that one night he got

angry and tried to communicate with it, but without success. "I don't get scared often," he says, "but that night I took the crucifix off the wall and slept with it."

At first, he was reluctant to share his experiences with anyone but his father. But then he told Mr. Howard, an elderly neighbor.

Mr. Howard told him that he, himself, had seen a few strange things in the vicinity, and that others had witnessed inexplicable occurrences. Mr. Howard seems to think there is a tie-in with Jean Lafitte and the treasure that is said to be buried there somewhere. According to legend, Lafitte and his pirates frequently traversed the Delahoussaye Canal, a twenty-feet wide waterway near Grand Marais, which flows down to Vermilion Bay and the Gulf of Mexico.

Jackie's father also has some interesting stories. Several years ago when the parish was constructing a bridge about a mile behind Jackie's house, the workers uncovered an ancient grave. They found a skull, a few remnants of clothing, and some bones. Whether it was the remains of a pirate or not, no one knows, but one of the workers kept the skull as a souvenir.

There's also the story about a man being hung from a tree. According to Mr. Howard, this incident set off some strange happenings. "Everyone around Grand Marais has seen the man who walks those fields and then disappears," he says. Jackie's father points out that the hanging took place about a mile from the bridge over the canal, in the opposite direction from the grave site.

Not long ago, Jackie and his father went over his property with a metal detector. They got a strong reading near the front door of the house, directly beneath the spot where Jackie parks his truck. Whatever it is seems to be rectangular (or casket-shaped, as someone observed) with dimensions about eight-feet long by two-and-one-half feet in width. They haven't dug it up yet, but plan to do so in the near future.

Curiously enough, Jackie's house—and whatever is buried beneath his pick-up truck—is almost exactly midway between the site of the hanging tree and the grave site, and these three locations form a straight line on the map. A neighbor with psychic abilities told Jackie that his truck had disturbed a spirit; Jackie said this was pure superstition and refused to park elsewhere.

Not long afterwards, Jackie was awakened one night by Joyce, who said she could feel something poking her in the back. At first he simply "brushed it off," but then, he says, "something poked me three times."

A few nights later, Joyce was awakened by the sensation of something or someone playing with her hair. Though she turned her head to the other side she still felt it. Opening her eyes, she saw a man's face in front of her. "It was just smiling at me," she says. "It didn't look like it was trying to scare me. It was a pretty smile. I couldn't scream.... Nothing would come out. I was hoping it was a dream, but I huddled close to Jackie and woke him up. I told him, 'There's a man in bed with us.' He sat up and had chills all up and down."

Jackie adds that he's been getting that feeling for about nine years now. In fact, he had been seeing things in that same room for about three weeks before Joyce saw the face. At first he didn't tell her because, as he says, "I didn't want to scare her." But then one night he reached over for the lamp, and, "when I turned, a hand came toward my face just like you see my hand now. I backed up and Joyce asked 'What's wrong?' And I told her a hand came to me like it didn't want me around."

Another time, he said something came at him with a knife. "I jumped up and swung at it, and I hit the clothes rack. But it was there. It was real. And I tried to hit it but couldn't."

All of this happened while Jackie's truck was parked over the spot where he thinks something is buried. Finally, he gave in and moved it. After that the disturbances stopped. Everything, he says, "except for the sound of the door slamming."

Jackie and Joyce are concerned that things might get worse if they talk about all the strange occurrences. They say that things really "kicked up" after they confided in a neighbor. "That Thursday, it was the air conditioner," says Jackie. "We were lying in bed and it's like someone just shook it. What was peculiar is that my dog didn't bark."

He walked outside to see if someone was playing a prank on them. No one was. So "I brushed that off too."

Friday night he and Joyce and the three kids had just sat down to eat when "the back door knob started turning, and it was like someone was shaking the door to come in. I got to that door and was outside within two seconds. Nothing there. And the dogs never barked. If there would be somebody there, they'd bark."

Saturday night was even worse. "It was the door again. Someone was trying to get in. This was the first time I ever saw Joyce scared. I gave her a gun and I got mine. I told her, 'Anything tries to come through that door, shoot.' I walked every inch of this property. I walked down the headlands. I went in the cane fields, but there was nobody."

The bed Jackie's grandmother gave him before she died also provides mystery in the Landry household. When he lived there alone he would occasionally hear it move: "I'd say 'nah,' and just brush it off, but it can't be the house or the wind because I built this house myself, and I've got nine-inch walls and I used two-by-six's. I'm sitting on ten inches of cement foundation."

At first he didn't tell Joyce about the bed. "But one night we were laying down and she said 'Jackie, you ever feel this bed move?' I said 'Yeah, I sure do.' It's like you can feel it rocking, it just sways."

Joyce agrees: "It feels like when I lived in a mobile home and when someone walked you could feel the bed shake. We thought maybe the train track could be making it move, but it's a mile away."

"It's not impossible," says Jackie, "but I used commercial-bag mix in this foundation—which is more rock—and the footings are two-by-two feet deep, so it's not just the house moving."

The ghosts—if there are ghosts haunting this house—also display some of the more typical behavior of mischievous spirits. Lights go on and off by themselves. Footsteps resound from the upstairs bedroom when no one is there. And, says Joyce, "The ceiling fan will be on nearly every morning although Jackie says he makes sure to turn it off at night."

The first time she found the fan on she blamed Jeremi, her son. But Jeremi hotly denied that he was the culprit. And Jackie says, "It's not a short 'cause I wired this house myself."

Joyce never told any of this to Christy, her eleven-year-old daughter, because she didn't want her to be frightened in her own home. But one night Christy said, "Mama, when I come home [from school] and when I get about half way to the house I hear somebody calling my name in the cane field."

Joyce told her it was just the wind blowing the cane because she has to come home from school that way, and it's a long walk.

Mr. Howard, the neighbor down the lane, also hears things: "I've been here seventy-five years and when I was a young man I used to go out till all hours of the night. When I'd come home—day or night—somebody'd call my name."

He says he's used to it now: "All I can do is answer, but there's never anybody there. Sometimes I see a man in my pasture, or I see him walking down the road. Over the years I've gone countless times to try to talk to this man, but he disappears." Jackie says that his brother, Dana, believes Mr. Howard: "Just the other day...Dana was here, and he saw this guy with a beard and what looked like an old army shirt...walking in front of my house. And he thinks to himself, 'Why is this person just out-of-the-blue walking here?' All the cane was cut so when he passed the corner of my property, Dana decides 'Well, I'm going to ask this guy what he's doing here.' He walks to the road, and that guy's gone!"

Dana was so shaken that he wouldn't stay at Jackie's place without all of the lights on, even the barn lights. "Man," he said, "there's something out here watching me!" Apparently Dana even saw eyes watching him from the same upstairs window that Jackie and Joyce are "drawn to" each time they return home.

The night Jackie and Joyce saw something move in that upstairs window when they were driving down the lane, Joyce said, "Oh Jackie, there's something up there."

Jackie went around to the back while she watched the front. They felt certain that whoever was up there would have to come through the front door or try to jump off the balcony. But nothing happened. "I was nervous and started crying," says Joyce. "We went back down the road and drove back to the house to see if we could see it again, or if it was just glare. We didn't see it again."

"But I saw it too," Jackie assures her.

All of these incidents have taken a toll on Joyce. She began having nightmares: "For two weeks every night I dreamed about this table [where Jackie saw the pirates] with dirty, filthy, scroungy-looking men waiting for Jackie to come home."

Jackie says she'd wake up screaming because she was certain they meant to kill him.

Even when Joyce is awake, she is not free from visions, sometimes unpleasant: "Pictures come up in my mind of me hanging by my neck from the ceiling beam in my bedroom."

A psychic told her that some spirits are malicious and harmful, others not; that it depended on whose spirit was there.

One day she cut her finger on her Bible. This startled and dismayed her. She equates the accident with the other bizarre activities in the house.

Jackie says that before he moved into the house he'd never broken a bone, even though he'd had an active sports' life in high school. Since 1980, however, he's broken one leg twice, the other once, an arm, a hand, and his neck—all in separate incidents....

Both Jackie and Joyce note changes in themselves. Says Joyce, "I'm basically a happy person, happy-go-lucky. I love people. But it got to where we couldn't even speak to each other. I told Jackie, 'I don't know who I am anymore.' Finally, we went for a walk by ourselves out in the fields and he told me he went through the same thing."

Jackie said that it got so bad that his family didn't want to see him anymore: "I was horrible to them. Finally, I grabbed hold and said, 'Nothing is going to rule me!' I started going to church regular. It wasn't till Joyce started going through that too that I realized, 'Well, there *was* something here and it wanted me to go.' It had accepted me...but now that Joyce and the kids are here, it wants them to go."

But the Landry's are not planning to go anywhere. "I've been here nine years," says Jackie. "It's like I fought something all the time. I'm not afraid of it. I never ran, and I'm not going to."

They do plan to dig up whatever is buried at their front doorstep. Both of them hope this will solve the riddle surrounding their property, or at least close the roving eyes of the pirates....

HOME TO STAY

Could a man's devotion to his home defy even death? The people who live in a house on Convent Street in Lafayette seem to think so. And for good reason.

The house was built in the 1930's; The man who built it died there in the 1950's. In life he couldn't afford the bank notes, so he and his wife lived in the rough-hewn basement and rented out the three-bedroom house above rather than leave it. In death it seems that his spirit also refuses to leave.

The location is in the heart of the Hub City, on grounds overgrown with ligustrum and camelia. Its basement windows seem to spy along ground level between the shrubs, like square, dark eyes observing my approach. Above them are double-hung windows with black frames and the remnants of rusty screens.

Approaching the entrance, I ascend thirteen concrete steps to a wooden wrap-around porch. The resounding of my footsteps is disquieting, as are the occasional creaks of loose boards. The place seems abandoned.

As there is no response to my knocking, I turn to leave, but am startled by the sudden appearance on the porch of a young man with green eyes and a broad smile. Mike Billeaud invites me inside. Unoiled hinges creak in protest as the door closes behind us.

Mike tells me he is a computer engineer student. He lives here with his cousin. But over the years the house has been home to other members of his family, including four brothers and a sister, all of whom are from Metairie.

Mike was warned about the house before he moved in, especially by his brother Beau, who told him in no uncertain terms that the place was haunted.

But Mike didn't believe in ghosts—not then. Not even when Beau told him about the time he was cutting grass and noticed a light burning in the basement. Beau shut off the mower, went inside, and turned out the light by unscrewing the bulb. But when he went back to his mowing, he noticed that all the basement lights had come on, including the one he had just turned out. Figuring that someone—or something—must be playing tricks on him, he removed all the bulbs and padlocked the basement door.

Mike's sister, Sally, was also beguiled with lights that would go off and on, or sometimes pop and burn out for no apparent reason. Though she was not the sort to accept supernatural explanations, she did confess that her dog displayed unusually disturbing behavior while staying in the house.

And on another occasion, every bulb in the house suddenly popped, causing Mike's brother, Andy, and his roommate some uncomfortable moments.

There are other manifestations. One night after a party, while Beau's roommate, Elliott, was relaxing on the living room sofa, the French doors between the living room and the dining room were suddenly flung open. But there was no one there—at least no one visible—to open them. Elliott was quite startled.

Beau's employment as a guitarist at a Lafayette restaurant occasioned another incident. He asked his girlfriend, Kathy, to go to the house to pick up his guitar and bring it to him at the restaurant. Suspecting nothing, Kathy drove to the house with a friend, unlocked the door and tried to open it. But the door wouldn't budge. Kathy said it was as though something was holding it from the other side. So she shoved some more, but to no avail. Then she stepped aside, exasperated, and called out, "Okay, Ghost, open the door!"

Incredibly, the door creaked open.

Entering, she flipped on the light switch, but much to her dismay there was no light. Maybe the bulb was burned out, she reasoned. Maybe! So the two girls, growing more concerned by the moment, made their way through the darkness to the bedroom where Beau had left his guitar. Flipping on the light switch there, they discovered that this also caused the light in the living room to come on—even though Kathy had since turned the living room switch to the "off" position.

Genuinely rattled now, and anxious to get out, Kathy began searching for the guitar. It was not atop the bed, even though Beau had specifically told her that it would be. She found it on the floor next to the bed. And the case was open, never mind that Beau always kept it closed. Kathy grabbed the guitar, case and all, and hurried out with her friend, not even bothering to turn out the lights. As she pulled away, she looked back just long enough to notice that the house was suddenly plunged into darkness. "It was as though a master switch had been thrown by some invisible hand," she said.

Another incident occurred one night while Beau and Kathy were watching TV in the living room. Beau was certain he heard someone walking up the concrete steps and onto the front porch. When the knock he expected at the front door failed to materialize, he got up to investigate. Looking through the glass-paneled front door, he saw no one, even though the porch was clearly illuminated by a street light. But the footsteps still echoed along the porch. Beau says it was as though someone had walked onto the porch, turned the corner, and stomped to the edge. Opening the door, he heard his phantom night-walker rushing down the front steps.

When Mike moved in, he chose the middle bedroom as his own, although the landlord had instructed him to avoid that room. This was probably because of a weak spot in the floor. The room had been used for storage over the years and was quite cluttered. Lying about were many personal items which had belonged to the original owners, including crucifixes, icons and Bibles. The walls were hung with several extremely large framed holy pictures, like giant guardians in a rubble sanctuary. Mike and brother Andy cleared the room and disposed of the less valuable items in a dumpster.

Later that day, while Andy was on the phone with his girlfriend, he heard the "call-waiting" signal of another caller. Answering, he got a fuzzy connection. "Hello," someone whispered, and then Andy found himself staring into a dead telephone.

A short while later the fluorescent light strips in the bathroom started flashing on and off. Andy, who was getting dressed at the time, rushed out of the bathroom to see what was going on. Moments later, every light bulb in the house exploded.

Then the phone rang. By the time Andy reached it, the ringing had stopped. Answering it anyway, he was startled to hear the familiar whisper again. But this time it called him by name. "Hello, Andy," the voice said. Andy says he was so shaken that he threw the phone down, got out, and didn't return home that night.

Andy felt certain there was a ghost in the house, and that he had incurred its wrath by disturbing its belongings. The following day he had a little chat with Mike: "Mike," he said, "we need to get that stuff out of the dumpster. Ever since we junked it, there are things going on that I just can't explain."

Andy and Mike retrieved the keepsakes, returning them to their shrine, and Mike decided against moving into the middle bedroom.

For a time everything seemed to settle down, but then one night Mike was awakened by a strange sound. He was sleeping on the living room sofa-bed at the time. Still half asleep, he connected the noise with that of the wind blowing a newspaper taped onto a broken window. Realizing that there was no such window in the house, he started to get up to see what was happening: "Just at that moment something froze my body," he says. "I couldn't move a muscle. I was trying to holler to Andy in the next room. I couldn't speak; I was just immobilized. It lasted a few seconds.... I don't know how long, but when it passed I saw this white flash in my eyelids."

Mike says he was unable even to force his eyelids open. When it passed he jumped up. Heart pounding, he rushed into the kitchen expecting to find it a wreck because the noise had been "like sheets and sheets of newspaper being balled up and thrown." Nothing was amiss. When he went back to bed he wondered if he had been asleep and just dreaming.

Mike's cousin, Steve, who shares the house with him, has also had some strange experiences. One night while packing his clothes to prepare for his offshore job, he heard the door-bell ring. "Coming!" he yelled. The bell rang again, and again Steve yelled that he was coming. Whoever was at the door should have easily heard him. But the bell went right on ringing as though someone desperately needed to get inside.

The bell finally stopped when Steve opened the door. But no one was there. At first Steve surmised that it was the work of a prankster, perhaps the same joker who had slammed the screen door on another occasion. But both times he made a thorough search of the house and found that he was quite alone....

But Mike says he sometimes gets a feeling that he's not alone. For example, when he's playing the piano he gets a certain chill—a chill that he's come to associate with the presence occupying the house.

Perhaps the most disturbing incident occurred one night when Andy was alone. The bed in which he was sleeping suddenly bounced up and down as if someone had kicked it from underneath. Andy sprang from the bed, turned on the lights, and threw off the bedspread to investigate. He found nothing—nothing in the bed and nothing underneath. He left the lights on and lay awake for about an hour, wondering what was going on. All was still. Could he have just imagined it? But when he turned out the lights, the bed bounced again, as though his invisible tormentor wanted to give one more sign of its presence.

Reflecting on his prior skepticism regarding the spirit world, Mike says, "Yeah, I believe in ghosts now.... We've never seen this ghost. He's never appeared. But there are stories of married couples who lived here and left because the women were afraid. Things happen to others besides my family."

Mike asks if I'd like to see the basement where the previous owners lived. We have to stoop to get through the entrance, and presently find ourselves in an uninsulated, drafty portion of the house that has little to offer in terms of physical comfort.

Neither does it offer much in the way of clues to the disturbances. Here and there are a few pieces of primitive furniture, an assortment of empty wooden chests, a single tarot card pinned on a beam, and a framed photograph of the man himself. Not much, but one suspects there's more in this basement than a few worldly possessions....

Mike agrees: "[The previous owner] went to a lot of trouble to stay in this house. I think that's what happened after his death. He's staying here for some reason."

THE SPIRIT OF BUTCHER SWITCH

It was late when Dianne (not her real name) arrived home that night in rural Lafayette Parish. The house was empty—supposedly—and yet when she opened the door she was greeted by a strange, whirring sound.

Dianne lives with her husband and son in a small, but well-kept Acadian-style house on Butcher Switch Road. She is a registered nurse at Lourdes' Hospital in Lafayette, where she works the night shift from three till eleven. Since her husband works in Houston during the week, her four-year-old son, Barry, stays at the hospital's day/night care facility while she is on duty. Barry was with his mother when the two of them returned home that night.

She laughs about it now, while we are sitting in her brightly lit living room with sun streaming through an open window and freshly cut flowers on the table. But it was midnight then, dark and lonely, and like any other young woman she was concerned about entering an empty house after being away all day.

"I walked in and I thought, 'My God! What is that?' I went into my son's room and saw that it was his driving machine—a toy thing, turned on by a switch, which runs on batteries. It was on the floor, and it was turned on. I didn't remember him playing with that toy at all that day. I had put it on the shelf. Several people at work told me later that batteries had surges of energy. So I figured, okay."

Dianne says she let it go at that. But then,

about a week later, she was awakened in the middle of the night by the same thing. Even then she didn't think a great deal about it. "I still wasn't convinced that we had a ghost or anything," she says, smiling.

But things kept on happening, nothing big, but just enough to cause Dianne to start wondering. For example, her brother-in-law lived in the same house with them for a year while he was going to school. He often reported hearing footsteps in the dining room, or the turning of the door knob. "I figured it was one of y'all," he told Dianne, "but I turned around and absolutely nothing was there."

Dianne smiles, brushes back a strand of dark brown hair, and says they all laughed about it. "My husband heard things too, but figured 'Well, it's probably that we built a new home and new homes settle.'"

Then there was the case of the flying brush. It happened right after Barry had hung up the phone from talking with his dad in Houston. As always, his dad had told him to give his mama "a big kiss and a big hug for me." So Barry and his mom were sitting on the bed hugging when suddenly, "My hair brush came flying out of the closet and hit the side of the bed. It came at an angle and a good distance."

It didn't just fall out, says Dianne, "It flew."

Turning to Barry, she said, "Son, did you see that?"

When Barry answered, "Mama, magic," she knew she wasn't just imagining things. So she called her sister. "I just couldn't take it anymore, so we spent the night at her house."

Dianne turned to her religion that night, by

reading the Bible and saying prayers, both of which made her feel stronger.

The next day her niece asked about the brush, so when they went back to the house they began looking. And looking. It was not where Dianne had last seen it. They finally found it in the closet, behind her purse on a shelf. "I didn't put it there!" says Dianne, emphatically.

The most recent incident was on Barry's birthday, which happened to fall on Halloween. Again they were awakened in the middle of the night by one of Barry's toys, a microphone on a stand, which was making a whining noise. It was his birthday gift. "I know I turned it off," insists Dianne.

Dianne finally talked to her pastor. "Things like that can happen," he told her. He also urged her to pray, saying that "Prayers can help."

It was a comforting suggestion, and one that fit in neatly with Dianne's own thoughts: "I feel the most likely explanation is that there are people who need your prayers. My father is dead and I believe it's possible he may need my prayers. The day the hair brush flew out, Barry and I had been talking about my father. Barry said, 'I don't want Paw Paw to be in heaven; I wish he would come here. That night it happened. That thought sent chills down me. I feel his presence."

THE HOUSE OF HISTORY

I am often asked if I have personally experienced the presence of a spirit. The answer is well, maybe—depending on how a spirit manifests itself. Certainly I have not been confronted by an apparition. But something peculiar happened during one of my interviews (see "The Ghost of Grand Prairie"). And then there was the chill that never left me.

It happened at the House of History in the old steamboat town of Washington, Louisiana. This is one of the homes on tour owned by Mrs. Mildred Nicholson, who works at the tourist bureau. There's a lot of history in her old antebellum home. There's also a ghost or two.

I had just started collecting ghost stories for this book when a friend from Broussard called to teli me of a scary experience she had there.

Rosie was showing her Yankee brother-in-law (from Pennsylvania) the sights around Acadiana. Driving up past Opelousas and on into Washington, they stopped at the tourist information office and inquired about which house had the most history. Mrs. Nicholson replied that her house probably did.

Rosie, remembering my research on this topic, asked if any of the homes on tour might have a ghost story or two. Again the answer was the Nicholson house. So, Mrs. Nicholson, who is quite an interesting person herself, closed up shop and agreed to show them around.

While touring the home, Rosie suddenly felt a pain in her left leg; as they continued, her face became hot and prickly, and her heart began to race. She felt so completely overcome that she had to leave the house immediately. Not until they were back in the car did the feeling leave her. Mrs. Nicholson told her that another guest had once experienced the same thing and had to return to the house to be rid of her ailment.

And, indeed, another acquaintance of mine, Bobbie Melancon of Carencro, told me of a similar discomfort while she was touring the house. First it was a chill, which came over her right after she noticed the blowing drapes in the front bedroom—although there was no breeze. Then it was a deep emotional sadness, followed by a pain in her leg, both of which came to her moments after she saw a mass of bluish fog in the basement.

Fortunately, both Rosie and Bobbie have completely recovered. But when they relate their stories to me, I immediately set off to see the house for myself.

What I find is a large, one-and-one-half story

house with a spacious front gallery, wide breezeway, and gunshots in the plaster walls. Mrs. Nicholson is a charming hostess, and readily answers questions about personal memorabilia, antiques, history and ghosts. She shows me a dazzling saddle with sterling silver adornments, as well as photographs when she was the first Miss Louisiana in 1931, and when she was an accomplished equestrian.

She tells me that the house was built in the early 1800's, and that it served as headquarters for both sides during the Civil War. The bloodstained upstairs floor is a gruesome reminder that it was also used as a hospital, and was the site of amputations and unimaginable sufferings. The cellar, protected by two-feet-thick brick walls, contains portholes which allow a person to defend himself during battle from the inside. And below ground are bones which attest to the failed attempts of the top floor ministerings.

But the most fascinating feature of the house is the one-legged soldier who dwells somewhere between the hospital attic and the basement fort. He's appeared several times to Mrs. Nicholson and her seventeen-year-old grandson: "At two a.m. I felt the presence of somebody in the house and I opened my eyes and saw him leaning over me," says Mrs. Nicholson. "He just appears and then leaves."

One night when her grandson was sleeping in the front bedroom, he called out to her. "Come quick!" he yelled. Mrs. Nicholson rushed into the room just in time to see the familiar form disappearing into thin air.

Another time Mrs. Nicholson says she heard an unmistakable creaking sound on the stairs. "I looked up and there he was at the top of the stairs. I froze and he disappeared."

I ask a question she's probably answered a hundred times before.

No, she replies, she is not afraid to live here alone: "You see, he's not that mischievous." She adds that when some people take a picture, a halo will appear on the photo, or it completely blanks out. I have heard this story before, from a friend who told me that his photograph of one of the rooms was impossibly flawed.

Mrs. Nicholson's daughter was very skeptical when first told of the spiritual occupant in the house. But that was before the time she tried to enter the front door and was held back by an invisible force. It was as though something was trying to tell her to become a believer.

During the tour, Mrs. Nicholson pauses and motions to the large bedroom to the left of the hall. She mentions that I might feel a different atmosphere altogether on entering: "If you feel goosie or have hot waves go over you, this is where the apparition comes. You can feel a difference. It's a heavy feeling.... I feel him now," she says, wide-eyed. "Look at my skin, he's all around me."

I feel nothing, but in my newly assumed role as ghost-hunter, I am determined to be open-minded. So I ask Mrs. Nicholson for permission to sit alone for awhile in the front bedroom.

I try to recall all the things I have heard about this room. There is a secret hatch in the floor which leads to the fort beneath, and which Mrs. Nicholson says was used for escape during the Civil War skirmishes in town. In the center is a table displaying newspaper clippings about the house. There is also a rare photograph of Union General Nathaniel Banks sitting on the front porch with the family of Gerard Carriere, the original owners. A remarkably good photo considering that it was taken in 1863.

Since this is also the room in which the spirit occasionally materializes, I place my tape recorder on the table, hoping to capture some audio sign of its presence. My imagination runs wild, and I wonder what I will hear. Or see. But there is nothing—nothing but the incessant ticking of a pendulum clock and the shadows of a tree at the screened windows.

I take a deep breath, sit back in the chair, and try to read some of the newspaper clippings. And still I wait. Surely something will happen. Something benign! But nothing does.

Not until I walk out onto the front gallery. Now a strange chill comes over me, and I shudder. Surely it's just the difference in temperature between a cool, drafty house and the heat of June.

But I am unable to shake the feeling of a chill in my left arm.

Months pass, and still the warmth in my arm does not return. I visit a psychic in connection with my research and learn that he is also a *traiteur*. He tries to rid me of this affliction. It seems to help, if only marginally.

Although the chill was unwelcome at first, it soon becomes my personal battle scar. In fact, it's as though I have been bestowed with some point of reference to detect a real haunting. Because now, when I enter a place where there is a soul at unrest, I can tell.

THE GIRL IN THE ATTIC

The townspeople of Washington tried to warn Gerry Morain about the old Carrington house. But she "flat refused to hear any of it" and went ahead and bought it anyway. It was the summer of 1984, and she and her family were far too delighted to be moving out of a modern, brick structure and into their "new" 118-year-old house to be concerned about ghosts.

Gerry, like Mrs. Nicholson a few blocks away, works outside the home. In fact, she is the proprietor of Patsy's Cafe on Main Street in this historic steamboat town. And, like Mrs. Nicholson, she is kind enough to leave work to give me a tour.

Like many of these old homes, this one had an unfinished attic when the Morains moved in, so

Gerry and her family began their own renovations, converting the attic into two bedrooms and a bath. That's when things began to happen: "Something just didn't want the top to be completed," she says, pointing in the direction of the stairs.

Gerry tells me that almost every day someone in the family would find certain items downstairs "which had been left upstairs the night before."

At first they thought they were imagining these things, or that someone was pulling a prank, so after a while they got each other to witness what they had left upstairs, and where. This confirmed their suspicions. Someone or something was in the house besides themselves.

Once the upstairs work was completed, things began to settle down. For a while. But then the patter of little footsteps began. Sometimes they could hear the sounds at night; other times in broad daylight. Even visitors heard the footsteps, which sound like those of a small child. Gerry says you can hear them most clearly while sitting in the living room beneath the attic bedroom.

I look upwards and notice the exposed beams high overhead. Wood everywhere—on the walls, on the floor, and on the ceiling. I imagine there must be lots of creaks and settling noises in such an old house with so much wood.

Yes, Gerry tells me in her pleasantly throaty voice, there is, but there's a big difference between normal creaking sounds and the "thump-thump-thump" of footsteps.

Then Gerry tells me about the apparition. It happened in January of 1985, about 1:30 at night when she was walking through the study toward her bedroom: "There's a closet in the study with a hidden door that opens underneath the stairwell.

The children call it 'the secret room' because you don't see that it's there...unless you're looking for it. The apparition came from the closet. It was a young child about eight-or ten-years-old, a white girl with long hair in a long dress, which tells me it was from way back. The vision that I saw was translucent. It appeared that the child went through the middle of the room, and she just disappeared...."

I ask Gerry about her reaction. "Well," she replies, smiling, "there's a funny feeling that comes over you. It's like every hair on your body stands on end; every pore of your skin is aware of something."

Was the apparition aware of Gerry's presence?

"I don't think so. She was gliding slowly. It seems like she was intent on making it across the room. For weeks after that I got up each night—I wasn't getting any rest—to try to see her again.... I was not afraid."

As for who—or what—it could be, Gerry tells me that her husband, while digging in the yard one day, uncovered some human bones beneath a layer of bricks. The bones were small, like a child's. He put the remains back and covered up the hole.

Could it be the bones of a little girl? Possibly, but Gerry isn't ready to draw any conclusions without further evidence. Toward that end she has traced the ownership of the house back to a man named Carrington, whose business was trading farm animals and slaves. Unfortunately, most of the records are so old and faded that they are almost impossible to read. Both of us wonder if the papers could be deciphered, and, if so, whether they would reveal anything about the girl in the attic—or in the yard.

THE DREAMIES

There are four occupants dwelling in a house in St. Martinville, but only one is visible to the human eye. The other three make themselves known mainly through the noise they make. The one you can see (let's call her Missy) seems to live alone in this modest but clean and comfortable house her parents built. But when I visit her on a warm, Sunday afternoon, she tells me that she shares her home with a tall man, a tall woman, and a young boy.

Missy, who is a very warm and likable lady, says she first became aware of their presence when things started going off and on by themselves, like the lights, the television and even the dishwasher. Then objects began to disappear. This happened countless times, says Missy, sighing, and was especially frustrating when it involved a favorite blouse, or personal jewelry.

Sometimes a search would turn up the missing items; sometimes not. At other times they would later be found right where they were supposed to be.

Once, when Missy's mother was still alive, the two of them were looking for a certain family recipe for Christmas dinner. It wasn't in the file box where it was supposed to be, though they had used it as recently as Thanksgiving. So they searched the house, looking in cabinets and drawers and other likely places, but all to no avail. Christmas eve came, and still no recipe. And then it was time for Midnight Mass.

Missy wanted to wear her new jacket to Mass,

her Christmas gift, though it was still beneath the tree. Her mother said no, and instead suggested that she wear the old cashmere coat with the little mink collar which was sealed in a bag and had been hanging in a closet for years. Although out of style, it was a perfectly good coat, so Missy reluctantly pulled it out of the closet, unsealed it with some difficulty, and put it on. She put her hand into the pocket and, *voila*, there it was, the missing recipe!

Missy calls her invisible houseguests the "Dreamies," a name first coined by her old aunt, who had some of the same experiences in the house. She says she doesn't so much see them "like I see you right here," as she "feels their presence." But then she goes on to explain that the woman is surrounded by an aura of turquoise blue. The man gives the impression of having on a tweed or plaid jacket. Both are tall and carry themselves upright, but the boy is slouched. "It's a force you can't give a human description to," she says, smiling.

"Do they appear together?" I ask her.

The answer is that sometimes they do; sometimes they don't. Their favorite place, she tells me, seems to be the loveseat in the living room. Missy has rearranged the furniture so that this piece is not seen from the entrance doorways.

And is she afraid to live alone?

"Well," she replies, "it did frighten me at first, but not to the point of wanting to move out. It wasn't that kind of fear."

Missy tells me about the night the Dreamies were making so much noise she couldn't sleep, and in her own bedroom! It sounded like rapid

pounding on the wall and the sound of people walking on a wood floor, though her room is carpeted. Since she had to get up and go to school the next morning—Missy is a teacher—she sat up in bed and scolded them. "You get out of here!" she yelled. "You can go and live in the back room, but this room is mine and off limits to you!"

Incredibly, the noise stopped. But just as incredible, the Dreamies seemed to take up residence in the back room. And they let people know that it was their room, as they did one night when Missy's aunt tried to sleep there. After an unsuccessful attempt, she ran out exclaiming, "Those Dreamies got me!" She said the bed felt as though it was being elevated, and "they" were patting her arm and stroking her hair.

Another aunt, who heretofore didn't believe in such things, also tried sleeping in the back room. She abandoned the attempt, however, when the sliding door leading into the room opened, and she saw "someone" standing there looking at her.

"Which one?" Missy inquired.

"The tall woman," replied the aunt.

Apparently, the Dreamies don't like intruders in their room, because so far they have permitted only a religiously devout godmother to sleep there in peace. But no one else, not even Missy's mother, and not even when she chose to sleep there after a quarrel with her second husband. She had no sooner turned in for the night than she was pulled out of bed by some invisible force and couldn't get back in.

"After that," says Missy, laughing, "it was much easier to make up with her husband."

And do the Dreamies ever become violent?

"Well, the day my sister got married, they were very upset." She says they began to knock things over, including her father's heavy chair, and making noises that sounded like luggage being thrown around.

Then there was the day they sent her a message, by ringing a bell in her bedroom on the day a friend died. When she heard about his death, she made the connection between the bell and his passing. She feels it had something to do with the fact that she had kept his letters in that same room.

On another occasion, just before her mother died, someone or something rearranged a scrapbook by placing everything in reverse order. The book, complete with photos and scriptural passages, was on the theme of life.

One day a customer in an adjoining beauty shop (which is just off the kitchen) commented to Missy's mother that it must be nice to have someone cleaning her kitchen when she was away. She said she could hear the sounds of cabinet doors opening and closing, the dishwasher being loaded, turned on and running. Yet no one was in the kitchen at the time.

Missy also tells me about her father, who was fond of both coffee and beer: "After Daddy died, we heard coffee being made, and we smelled coffee every day at five-thirty as usual, and often times we'd hear the sound of a beer top being popped."

And does Missy have an explanation for all these disturbances?

"We think we're starting to get some answers," she replies. She goes on to explain that she and her sister have discussed the possible correlation to her older brother's death at age fourteen, a deceased aunt, and her father's passing.

Several months ago, when her mother was in the hospital, the Dreamies were unusually quiet, and there's been no sign of them since her death: "It's like when you're used to something being there, you notice when it's gone."

Missy also suggests that they may not want to frighten her now that she's alone in the house. "But they're here," she hastily adds, "they're just not going to bother me."

ADDIE AT SUSIE

It was the middle of the night; and the middle of her dreams. Or so thought Mary Lee Wicks when the knocking began at the upstairs back door. As reality dawned she realized that the knocking was real. Not to worry. It was her husband's custom to come up the back porch stairs when he got home late at night. He'd knock softly so as not to wake the kids, and Mary Lee would get up to open the door.

But no one was there when she went to the door. Could the entire thing have been a dream? It seemed so real.

Several nights later, she heard three distinct knocks. This time she knew it wasn't her husband because he was already at home. In fact, when she got up to investigate, she found him trying to coax their seven-year-old daughter, Lydia, back to bed. The knocking had awakened the entire household.

The Wicks' family lives at Susie Plantation on Highway 182 past Franklin between Garden City and Centerville. Built in the gracious antebellum style of other fine sugar plantations along the Teche, it has galleries in front and back—the back, of course, being the front in pre-Civil War days when the Teche was the main highway.

Mary Lee, an attractive lady with shoulder-length brown hair, has been researching the history of the place. She says the house was built in the early 1800's. The plantation once extended to banks on both sides of the Bayou Teche. Court records show a long list of slaves, animals, vehicles of conveyance and other goods claimed as assets by the original owners.

Stories abound that someone hung himself there. And since the house was on the main line of march for three destructive Union invasions, it was doubtless the scene of Yankee depredations, possibly even skirmishes and death. Also there is the above-ground tomb of Addie E. Harris near the house, whose marker indicates that she died in 1872 at the age of 22.

The Wicks are not the only residents to notice the strange happenings. A previous resident said the living room was always cold and hard to heat in winter and she felt uneasy in the room. She also related to the present occupants a story that remains unexplained.

One night she and her son heard a thumping noise that became louder and louder. Arming themselves with a gun and a baseball bat, the two descended the old wooden stairs, ready to defend their home against what sounded like someone attempting to break in. The noise started in the front bedroom but seemed to centralize beneath the stairs in the hall closet.

In spite of their search, they could not find the source; but neither did the noise stop. So they called the sheriff's department for assistance. When the officers arrived, everything grew quite. As soon as they left, however, the infernal racket started again, and continued until dawn.

Another previous resident—let's call her Betty—also heard what sounded like someone walking and creeping along the steep stairs, but she says the sounds would stop whenever the lights were switched on. She also noticed an increase in activity when she cleaned off the old grave of Addie Harris. Whenever Betty replaced the flowers, however, the house would become peaceful. As a result, she and the other residents affectionately refer to the disturbance as "Addie."

"I would be working in the yard and stop at her grave to say a prayer for her," Betty recalls. "And I would tell her 'How beautiful your house is!' And when the footsteps would start, I'd say, 'Addie, I'm not going to hurt your house, I'm cleaning it.'"

One time when Betty was carrying a wicker basket of laundry upstairs, she tripped twice and almost fell down the stairs. But "something," she says, caught her.

She and Mary Lee both noticed another peculiarity. The hall door would not stay closed, although recent renovations had made the door level.

Says Mary Lee: "I'd pass and the hall door would be open. So I'd close it and when I came back it was open again."

This is the door to the closet beneath the stairs where it is said the three children who lived there in pre-Civil War days had their playroom.

Mary Lee's hazel eyes sparkle, and she laughs as she tells about the time her kids had friends over to spend the night. They all slept in the living room and Mary Lee was in the downstairs front bedroom:

"About one or two in the morning I heard someone falling and stumbling on the stairs. I thought, 'Oh no, one of the kids has gotten up to go to the bathroom and has become disoriented!' But when I got up to check, all of the kids were sleeping. I had a little trouble getting back to sleep that night."

On two occasions Mary Lee thought she had seen someone walking on the upstairs gallery outside her bedroom. But she told no one about it, at least not at that time.

Then her seven-year-old daughter, Lydia, woke up one night to find a lady with black hair standing at the foot of her bed. Though Lydia tried to awake Mary Lee, she said she could not, so she "just closed her eyes tight and went back to sleep." In the morning she told Mary Lee about her strange visitor.

Mary Lee says she didn't make a big deal of it at the time, but she did ask how the lady was dressed. Lydia answered that the woman was wearing a red dress with "drapey stuff hanging down from the sleeves."

That's when Mary Lee began questioning the

previous residents of Susie to find out if anything unusual had ever happened to them.

One of them told her about the time that relatives of yet another previous owner had come through town and stopped by for a visit. These visitors had some old photos of portraits which had once hung in the home. Incredibly, one of the portraits was of a lady with black hair *and wearing a deep red dress with draped sleeves.*

The Wicks have since had their home blessed, and are seldom disturbed by strange noises. But now and then when they do hear something, they good-naturedly quip, "It's just Miss Addie."

And on the grounds outside, beneath the moss-covered live oaks, there's an inscription atop the crumbling brick structure of Addie's grave. "Weep not," it reads, "for she is not dead. She is only sleeping."

THE SPANISH TRAIL SPECTRE

I take the Old Spanish Trail west from Crowley, cross over the railroad tracks, and follow a dusty, winding drive to the Ziegler's tree-nestled home. It is not what I expected. Instead of a large Victorian-style home looming out of the mist, complete with peeling paint and broken shutters, I come upon a cozy brick home built along traditional lines—not exactly the kind of place for so many inexplicable occurrences. But it is an ideal setting for their family business, the Spanish Trail Nursery.

Jeannie Ziegler, the lady of the house, thinks she knows why so many strange things happen here. The land was once an Indian reservation, and after that it was the site of two other houses (at different times). One of the houses burned, and rumor has it that a small boy died in the blaze. The other house was abandoned because, as Jeannie says, "so many bad things happened."

Not all members of the family put credence in such stories—or in subsequent happenings. Jeannie's husband, "Teeny," for example, believes there are logical explanations for all the strange goings-on. So does their son, Manuel. But both have had an experience or two that defies logic.

On the other hand, the women of the home seem to be sensitive enough to receive and accept such things as visions and voices, and are willing to talk about their experiences.

Jeannie and her oldest daughter Trina—now married and living away—lead me into the den to continue our conversation. Jeannie pulls back an area rug to show where tiles buckle and pop off the floor. She believes an old water well might have been there; now she calls it "the archways to the devil's den."

At this, Trina jumps into the story with accounts of shuffling feet along the carpet in the girls' bedroom, which she says have been heard repeatedly by many people. Once, when the room was dark and the girls were ready for sleep, someone—or something—seemed to shuffle over and sit on the edge of their bed, making an impression in it. She and her sisters screamed, and when their mother rushed in, the disembodied intruder got up and shuffled away. Afterwards, Trina refused to sleep in the room. She says that her friends were so frightened after spending a night there that they wouldn't come back.

And there are other things, for example an antique rocking chair that sometimes rocks by itself. "Must be the air conditioning or something," Mr. Ziegler says. Jeannie smiles, shakes her head, and tells me that her mother, another skeptic, was once sitting in this very chair when she noticed a woman wearing a long dress walking down the hall. Thinking it was Mrs. Ziegler—Teeny's elderly mother—heading toward the boys' room, and concerned that she might need assistance because of her age, she got up and followed. But there was no one there, not in the boys' room and not in the hall.

"I hear voices, too, which no one else hears," says Jeannie. The voices are muffled, and the only thing she has ever been able to make out was a man's voice repeatedly saying, "The trees are beautiful out here."

On this, all can agree, because the trees adjacent to the house and in the surrounding pasture truly are beautiful. But that doesn't explain the sounds of a crying baby, which the children sometimes hear while standing near the kitchen stove.

On three occasions, Jeannie has seen a young boy in the yard through the kitchen window. Each time, he appears closer to the house. One day she walked outside to ask who he was and why he wasn't in school. But the boy was gone. Disappeared! Jeannie finds it odd that he would even be on their property in the first place, since it is in such a remote setting. She also wonders why he would wear shorts on such a cool October morn, and why he just stands there staring out past the house....

Occasionally, she hears a horse galloping across the front gallery at night. Other people have also seen or heard horses, including Robert Ziegler, a cousin, who came by one day for a visit and commented about "the horse running in the yard." A quick check revealed nothing, not even a track.

Another time, when Jeannie was in the bedroom, she heard what sounded like a horse galloping on the front porch. Looking out her window, she was startled to see a red ball of light *(feu follet)* that came at her through the window. "I got up and ran out of there fast!" she says.

Jeannie and another daughter, Dana, both seem to have a touch of ESP. They say there's a bit of Cajun folklore to explain that, too. Premature babies are supposedly born with a "second skin," a veil which is related to this gift. Both Jeannie and Dana were "premies."

Jeannie's husband complained one night that the children were disturbing his sleep, that it was too late for them to be up playing and making so much noise. They seemed to be rushing in and out of their bedroom, at the same time slamming doors against the bed. After repeated requests for them to stop—followed by no response—Jeannie finally got up to look in on them. All were sound asleep—all except Jeannie and her husband....

A tennis-sized ball came bouncing down the hall one day all by itself. The statue of the Blessed Virgin was found moved—twice. The master bedroom is admittedly chilly and there's a strong smell of flowers at times.

Jeannie and the children were startled one night by a terrible scream from the master bedroom. Worried about Mr. Ziegler, who was in this room, they all rushed in to find him sitting up in bed and sweating. "It's all right, kids," he said, "I just had a bad dream." But he confided in his wife that he had not been sleeping, that he'd had a terrifying feeling of being physically held down and unable to get up!

The family dog, "Amber," even reacts to unseen things, sometimes with a perky look and wag of the tail, as if someone welcome is approaching; at other times he reacts with a growl as if being disturbed.

Manuel was outside one day and heard a noise inside the house that sounded like glass bottles being moved. When he went inside to investigate, he found the house empty.

Perhaps "Big Foot" figures into the picture. Once, while Manuel was playing outside the plant nursery, he saw a huge furry animal. He jumped up on the car and yelled for his sister to "get in the house and tell Dad to bring the shotgun!" But as the family rushed out to see, the animal leaped the fence and dashed into the surrounding forest.

Not long afterwards, the Ziegler's awoke one morning to find a large pile of manure on the front porch. A series of tracks were nearby. They took pictures, as well as specimens of the droppings, and showed them to an agriculture specialist in the hope that he could identify the culprit. He could not. It wasn't from anything known to him, neither human nor animal. In the meantime, trackers reported that the creature was probably still on the property as the tracks led nowhere.

As I leave, Mr. Ziegler points to the elegant black iron fence that surrounds the property and borders the drive. It came from the old cemetery in Crowley, he says, adding that, there, it was meant to keep the spirits in; whereas, here, it's meant to keep the spirits out.

I suggest that it may not be working so well. Jeannie agrees.

PRISSY AND PUSSY

Could a little lady with her white cat be haunting this three-story colonial on Main Street in New Iberia? And what about the noises? Or the television sets that go off and on? Or the footsteps?

It certainly doesn't look haunted, not with its fresh paint, shuttered windows and neatly manicured lawn. But nineteen years ago it was a different matter. Then it was vacant and somewhat run-down in appearance, with overgrown surroundings and in need of paint.

That's when Connie (not her real name) came along. Connie is an independent businesswoman, intuitive, energetic and pretty. Even though she lived in north Louisiana at the time, and wasn't looking for an old house, she was drawn to the place, and decided it would make a good investment. Thus, for the next several months, she and her husband spent their weekends in New Iberia repairing, painting, and otherwise renovating. When they finished, they had four efficiency apartments to rent out.

But before they finished, they began to understand why the house had been vacant for so long. The first hint came on a weekend when Connie was alone in the house. She was scrubbing the wooden floor of the sunroom on the second story. The front door was closed and locked: "I heard someone come in, close the door, walk up the stairs and come up behind me."

Connie turned around expecting to see her husband there, or maybe some other member of the family. Someone with a key to the front door. But no one was there. Genuinely mystified and not a little frightened, she went downstairs and looked around. Nothing and nobody. In fact, the door was still locked.

Connie looks at me, smiles, and brushes back a lock of light brown hair before going on in a matter-of-fact tone: "I thought 'Boy! I'm really hearing things!'"

So back upstairs she went, and back to work. But again she heard the door open and close, the footsteps on the stairs, and the noise behind her—not once, but several times: "I thought, 'This is ridiculous!' So finally, without turning around, I said, 'I don't know who you are, but I hope you came to help, because I'm really busy. I love this home, and I'm trying to take care of it. So I hope you help me instead of hindering me.'"

The rest of the day was quiet, says Connie.

That night when her husband came home—they were staying at Connie's parents' house—he sat down on the edge of the bed, wide-eyed, and said to her, "I don't know how to tell you this...but our house is haunted." It seems that he had gone to the house later that day and heard some strange noises—the sound of the front door being opened and closed, footsteps on the stairs, and someone walking up behind him.

A few days later it was the painter's turn for a scare. Connie's husband had come into the house to find him terrified. Someone—or something—he claimed, had come over and touched his leg while he was on the ladder. Said he: "I went down and I locked that door and I got back on the ladder. They came in the door and walked up the stairs and touched me again. I ain't painting no more by myself in this house. No sir! It's haunted!"

Finally, when the house was finished and they began renting out the apartments, neither Connie nor her husband mentioned these incidents to their tenants. Perhaps they should have, because the first two couples who lived there suddenly moved out without an explanation. It wasn't until several years later that Connie saw some of these former tenants and learned what happened. They, too, had encountered a strange presence in the house, and been frightened away.

Another couple complained about their television sets going off and on, and doors that would lock and unlock by themselves. And another tenant said she came home one day to find "a little old lady" standing just inside the door. Her gray hair was pulled back and tied in a bun, and she wore a brooch at her neck.

Connie wonders if the little old lady could be Miss Prissy, the original owner of the house. She's suspected it for years, ever since she learned about the "little white animal" which she occasionally sees. She thinks it's a cat, though she's never really had a good look. When she told her husband, he dismissed it as the reflection of light.

"Well," says Connie, "I bought that explanation—kind of. And then one day I met this lady who said her friend had come here and seen Prissy's ghost and her white cat." The lady told Connie that Prissy and her cat were inseparable.

After asking around, Connie learned that other people had seen this elusive cat, including her sister, who didn't say anything because she didn't want to frighten her.

When Connie and her husband decided to move back to New Iberia, they tore down the walls dividing the house into apartments and moved in themselves. Again the old house was filled with the sounds of hammers and saws and smell of sawdust.

The painstaking restorations are almost complete. Connie and her husband are careful to recreate the authenticity of the era. Though Connie's interests are mainly in arts and antiques—with which she has filled the house—she's also researching the history of the place.

And what about Miss Prissy?

"Well," says Connie, "one day we had company, and my son came running downstairs into the dining room where we were eating and excitedly asked, 'Mom, were you just on the stairway to my room?'

"When I said I wasn't, he said, 'Oh, my God, I just saw Prissy for the first time!'"

THE GARDENING GHOST

Mr. C. is a professional educator at the University of Southwestern Louisiana. At first he is reluctant to grant an interview, saying his colleagues would either tease him mercilessly or think him crazy if his experiences appear in print. He finally agrees on condition that I not reveal his name. We meet in the campus library, not far away from his place of work, and take a seat at a table. He tells me his story in a quiet, studious manner.

The house where he lives appeared at first to be just an ordinary Lafayette house, but it was anything but that. Mr. C. rented the place in 1981. He had hardly moved in before he began hearing strange noises: doors opening and closing, even a pantry door, which was off its hinges and had to be slid open. This particular door made a distinct grating noise and was unmistakable. The same was true of the front door. It opened and closed with a metallic click. Yet there was never anyone to be found near these doors.

Not long thereafter, Mr. C. began seeing strange things. First it was a woman, a white, shadowy figure working in the garden outside his bedroom window. She was there almost every night, and he could see her clearly, though there was something unreal and ethereal about her appearance.

About a year later, he awoke in the middle of the night to find an elderly couple standing at the foot of his bed. He blinked his eyes as one does when first awakened. But when reality struck, he

quickly reopened them and found the couple still standing there, staring at him.

The woman was small, he says, with closely cropped, curled hair. She wore a white blouse and straight skirt. Her companion, a man with a potbelly, was dressed in a white, squared-off shirt, which he wore, untucked, over dark pants. Even as Mr. C. watched, the couple rose in the air, floated toward the ceiling, and disappeared.

Bewildered more than terrified, Mr. C. questioned his landlord about the house, in the course of which he described the couple and the lady he had seen working in the garden.

The landlord listened attentively, then told Mr. C. about the old couple who had died in the house. The descriptions matched. It seems that the man was terminally ill, and had been brought home from the hospital to die in his own bed. After his death, the woman had trouble sleeping, so she gardened every night! She died later in her rocking chair.

MYSTERIES AT JEFFERSON ISLAND

Acadian folklore has it that if a person builds a home late in life, he will not live out the year he begins the project. Perhaps that's the reason Joseph Jefferson never slept in the opulent house he built on Jefferson Island near New Iberia in 1870. He was age forty at the time, not so old by current standards, but an advanced age in 19th Century America. So Jefferson, for this reason, spent his nights behind the mansion in a quaint dwelling called the Cottage.

Born in 1829, Jefferson was an architect, artist and author, as well as the famous Rip Van Winkle actor. He had an avid interest in spiritualism, which he pursued in order to communicate with his late first wife. It was said of him that he performed on the stage right up until the last days of his life.

Jefferson knew beauty when he saw it. The island that took his name—before that it was called Orange Island, Miller's Island, and Dupuy's Island—sits atop a massive salt dome arising from the flat, surrounding countryside. About twelve hundred acres in size, it is characterized by hills, valleys, plains, bluffs and forests, and overlooks a beautiful lake called Peigneur (or Simonette on earlier maps).

After Jefferson's death in 1905, his island and the magnificent ten-thousand square foot house he built passed through a succession of owners. Until 1980 the place was owned by the Bayless family. They donated the house and grounds to set up the Live Oak Gardens Foundation, a private, non-profit organization. The house is now open to the public.

Over the years there have been many stories of ghosts, apparitions and other unworldly happenings on Jefferson Island. There are accounts of a wispy form walking from one room to another, and of a headless woman in the skylight airwell, and strange noises and smells.

One of these is related as the cover story of the Sunday, Times-Picayune Magazine of August 30, 1925, complete with an artist's illustration. In it, Mr. Bayless himself gives an account of the time he was a child and saw a man in a top hat leaning over his bed. One of the man's hands was against a dresser, but the man was floating up in a glowing light. Bayless said the family hounds were howling away at the time.

In more recent years, housekeepers and tour guides have been repeatedly embarrassed and frustrated to find wrinkled beds in rooms where no one has been sleeping. Sometimes sheets go sailing away when they try to make up these beds. This is particularly the case in the Cottage. One day a mosquito net was pushed aside as though by some invisible hand, and the impression of a sitting person appeared on the bed covers. Doors are hard to open at times, just as though an unseen person is holding them closed. And sometimes the rocking chairs start rocking all by themselves.

THE COTTAGE

Mike Richard is the manager of Live Oak Gardens on the island. A good-humored man, he smiles when talking about the night he slept alone in the Jo Jefferson house. "I was acting as caretaker, and there was no one else on the premises at the time. I woke up and it was absolutely dark.... Couldn't see a hand in front of my face. But I could see a glow up on the ceiling in the corner. And I could hear heavy breathing coming from that direction. I sat up and just stayed real still and tried not to breathe so I could hear. It never moved. It just stayed in that same place. I'd say I listened to it for an hour."

Mike lives next to the main house in a building popularly referred to as the "Camp." He explains that it was built in the 1920's to accommodate guests because of transportation problems to New Iberia.

Listening to Mike talk in his down-to-earth manner, and hearing of his fascination with local and area history, it's easy to understand why he's so highly regarded by co-workers. He smiles again as he tells me about the time his young son encountered an apparition in the house: "He woke up one night and he could sense something. Then he saw an old man looking in the crib at his sister. The man's feet weren't touching the ground." Mike adds that his son, who was seven at the time, is "a very realistic kid; not a dreamer."

Roy Patout, a New Iberia sugar cane farmer with a dry wit and friendly manner, has also had some strange encounters on the Island. He and his wife, Ticky, live nearby, so I drive out to their lovely home for a chat. Ticky, who is a delightfully interesting character herself, shows me her collection of voodoo dolls, and regales me with stories of witchcraft, grandchildren, and their recent visit to haunted castles in Europe.

But it is the stories of Jefferson Island that I have come to hear, so Roy tells me about the time he was doing some repair work at the big house. It was dusk, and he was alone: "I walked into the hall, closed the front door and went into the dining room. There was a light on the floor. I thought it might be a car in the parking lot with a mirror, reflecting. I didn't think of anything like a ghost."

Roy started walking away, but as he moved, the light moved with him: "So I went to the window and looked outside to see if some fool was playing a trick on me with a flashlight. There were no cars in the parking lot—just my truck parked there. There was no reflection from the sun coming off the truck. I turned and walked into the hall. When I got into the hall, the light was there—like it was waiting for me."

Roy leans back in his chair and laughs, and his dark eyes seem to sparkle as he tells how it dawned on him that there was no window in the hall, no source for the light: "So where was the light coming from? I closed all the doors. It became pitch dark. But the light was still there. And then it got cold. Real cold! They say when it gets cold that's when they start appearing to you. I said, 'Uh-uh! This Cajun ain't gonna stay around here waiting for *nothing* to appear!'"

Roy doesn't say he dashed away, terrified, but he does admit to not bothering to close the front door on his way out.

The next morning he told Mr. Bayless about his experience. Replied Bayless: "You were fortunate. It only shows itself to certain people—at a certain time."

Roy also tells me about the expensive alarm system that had to be done away with. It was sensitive to temperature changes and was going off almost every night, causing the police and fire departments to respond to several false alarms. The alarm company put in what they called a "Ghostbuster," but that didn't work either. Now the property is protected by armed guards.

Back at Jefferson Island, I learn that some of the old timers in the vicinity think the Cottage is haunted by an old man who died there in the 1920's. He had been sitting on the porch in a rocking chair when he died, and his body remained there for several days before it was discovered. This was in the days before a salt mining operation was established, and the Island was a very isolated place.

Ever since, there have been numerous reports of unexplained activities. Mike Richard tells me about the man who went in one day to pick up the waste in the Cottage: "He closed the kitchen door after he walked in and he heard the spring on the screen door squeaking. He looked back and saw the screen door open and close as if someone had followed him in. But there was nobody there. He would never go back after that." Mike says that people who work there now "hear footsteps walking around."

Mike also relates the story of the 1928 discovery of buried treasure. A work crew was digging in an area shown on the map as Voodoo Land. They unearthed three brick triangular boxes with lead covers. The foreman, a *traiteur* called Daylight, gave the workmen the rest of the day off. The next day Daylight was gone; so were the contents of the boxes.

Rumor has it that the boxes were filled with gold and silver coins from Jean Lafitte's excursions. If so, Mr. Lafitte certainly got around, as the stories of his "buried treasure" seem to turn up all over south Louisiana. But it's also possible that the treasure dates from the time of the Civil War, when residents all over the state buried their money and other household valuables in advance of the invading Yankees. And, indeed, the Federals did make a raid on the place—it was called Dupuy's Island at the time—and carried away oranges, cigars and livestock.

In any case, Mr. Bayless' father was able to buy some of the coins back. They are French, English, and Mexican in origin. Mike has some of these coins in his possession at Jefferson Island.

The site of the treasure is also the setting for another story. There was a man called "the butler" who used to cut wood in that area for the fireplace. Each time he went out he claimed to hear chains rattling in the trees. He would not go out after dark.

Several tour guides in the Jefferson home have heard voices and slamming doors and footsteps in the rooms upstairs, even when they are there alone. Jane Wadsworth is one of them, but she is hesitant about discussing such things with visitors. She does, however, admit to having an encounter that went beyond simply hearing things: "I was on the second floor cleaning in the Camelia Room and I definitely sensed that someone was in the room with me. When I looked up I could see a pair of pants like someone standing there. I looked again and it was gone."

Bob Theriot of Delcambre works in the gardens. He came to the house early one morning to install a sink. When he crawled underneath the house he heard someone walking on the floor above him, as though pacing back and forth. He went up to see who it was. No one was there. Returning to his plumbing, he continued to hear the footsteps. Bob still wonders who was pacing the floors that day.

Perhaps the most volatile activity on the island takes place in the cafe. Joyce and Shirlene, sisters who work there, cite a long litany of bizarre activities, for example, beer bottles that crash to the floor all by themselves. Or paper cups that spew all over the room as if someone were flinging them one by one. "Like someone just had a hi-oh good time," says Joyce. She fled the room when the cups started flying, and returned after all was quiet.

THE JEFFERSON ISLAND CAFE

Then there are the voices. "We hear voices you can't account for," says Shirlene. "At first we thought it was some of the workers trying to spook us. But there's no one but us two and we both hear these voices. We just look at each other. We hear someone playing in the plastic forks or slamming down a tray on the floor. You'd no sooner get up to go back there and it'd stop."

Shirlene also says she's been touched a couple

of times on the shoulder. "But only Joyce was there and she was across the room and swore she didn't touch me."

Joyce tells me about the "terrible odor" in the video room. She says tourists often complain, but no source can be found.

One night Shirlene took a picture of five employees who had gathered in the cafe after work. But the developed photograph showed *six*. Joyce appeared to be sitting in the sixth person's lap, though she was sitting in a chair alone. "He looked Spanish," explains Joyce, "with a goatee. We could just see his face...It had a greenish tint."

Another time Shirlene answered the phone to hear someone whisper, "Get out!" The mysterious caller repeated his message three times. "I had goose flesh all over," she says.

Joyce remembers one especially peculiar night when she and Shirlene were waxing the floor after everyone had left. Finishing, they turned out all the lights. "We both commented on how pitch black it was because we had to walk to our car and we were all alone on the island. We got to the car and looked back and it was all lit up."

Joyce can laugh about it now, but she concludes by saying, "We weren't about to go back in there, though."

All these incidents pale into insignificance by comparison with the strange accident that occurred there on November 20, 1980. The workers on a Texaco drilling rig out on Lake Peigneur, just below the Jefferson home, apparently drilled into a salt mine deep below the surface. The effect was that of unplugging an enormous bath tub. The entire rig was sucked into the hole, as were a barge and all the water in the lake. And the water from a bayou that normally drains out of the lake began rushing backwards, creating turbulence for miles downstream.

Was there a supernatural connection? Old Jo Jefferson might know. Or the man on the porch in the rocker. But they're not talking.

THE PHANTOM OF POIRET PLACE

Poiret Place, near Plaisance, is probably the oldest house in St. Landry Parish. Slave-built in 1771 for a cotton merchant, this 5500-square-foot structure sits on 19 acres of beautifully landscaped land that was acquired through a Spanish grant. It was used as a hospital during the Civil War, and later as a girls' boarding school.

Today, this magnificent antebellum plantation is the home of Dr. Richard J. Bidstrup, M.D., a calm, soft-spoken man who practices medicine in nearby Opelousas. He lives there alone—unless, of course, you consider one friendly ghost.

I call on Dr. Bidstrup at his office in Opelousas, though I had previously seen and photographed his house from the outside. One of his colleagues, John Allgood, is present during the interview.

Dr. Bidstrup begins his story by pointing out that since his house is large and he lives there alone he often has house guests. One of them was John Allgood, who, on a Christmas night several years ago, was awakened by the sounds of footsteps on the third floor and set off to investigate. Dr. Bidstrup also heard "definite footsteps" and went out to see, but with pistol in hand. The two men met in the living room and continued their search together. They found nothing.

Another visitor reported hearing someone playing ping-pong on the third floor. But, again, a search turned up nothing.

"They kept telling me there was a ghost in the house," says Dr. Bidstrup, "but I didn't believe in ghosts."

But that was before the morning about ten or twelve years ago, at maybe three or four a.m., when he was awakened by a strong feeling of a presence in the room: "A very definite feeling of a presence. There was an image of a face at the foot of my bed. It was an elderly man, graying beard; wrinkled, deep-set eyes. An attractive person."

Dr. Bidstrup says he has been awakened in the night many, many times with this feeling of a presence—of somebody there.

Then there are the noises at Poiret Place. Dr. Bidstrup says it sounds as though people are walking outside his bedroom—up and down the stairs.

I ask him what he thinks is making the noise.

"A ghost," he replies without hesitation.

And do they disturb him?

"Not at all, he says. If they did I wouldn't live there." I live there by myself."

AN AUGUST AURA

Walking along Main Street in New Iberia, my hometown, I come upon the old LeBourgeois building, a turn-of-the-century, two-story structure with a few modern trappings. The ground floor, currently occupied by the Lagniappe Cafe, is covered with glossy black ceramic tiles. Above are a series of tall, verticle-opening windows. A sign tells me that it houses Creation Studios, owned by commercial photographer Kent Hutslar. From outward appearances the LeBourgeois building could be just another building on any Main Street anywhere in America.

But there is a difference. Perhaps it began on the day many years ago when someone buried a body in the ground beneath the floor. Who or why, no one knows; neither does anyone know the identity of the deceased. But workmen came across the skeleton in the early part of this century when the building was being converted into an automobile showroom.

Predictably, the discovery set off a blizzard of speculation. Some said it was the body of an unruly slave; others thought it might be a damnyankee; or maybe even an unfaithful husband (or wife).

Whatever the circumstances, the excitement soon settled down, and, except for occasional whispers about noisy ghosts, nothing out of the ordinary was known to have happened there. At least not when it was used by Isaac Martin—father of contemporary photographer Carrol Martin—for his photography studio. Nor when it progressed through a succession of tenants—from a doctors' offices to a babys' clothing shop and on to Stagg Records.

But when Kent Hutsler opened his studio in the upstairs portion of the building, things began to happen. Most of the activity occurs in the darkroom, which is located in a back corner office that had been closed off and neglected for many years.

Kent thinks he knows why it was closed off, and he offers to take me on a tour of the place. I meet him downstairs in the cafe—after hearing a few chilling stories about the building from the proprietress—and follow him out the door to the Main Street entrance. We climb a steep stairway and follow a long, oak-floored corridor with doorways on both sides. Along the way, he tells me about the "presence of an entity," which he can sense in the darkroom. He says that dogs would not go into that particular section, even when led on a leash.

Kent, a very tall man in his mid-thirties, strokes his dark beard and gestures toward the windows as he talks: "I'm notorious for working at night. When downtown goes quiet, it's my town.... I come up and sit in these windows. At one or two, a.m., New Iberia's like a ghost town. There would be this feeling of someone being with me...but turn around and nothing would be there."

Curiously enough, the proprietress of the Lagniappe Cafe had told me a similar story only a short time before.

Kent goes on, telling me about the night an "energy field" suddenly materialized in the doorway of the darkroom. He says it was a white glow, with no particular shape that could be identified as human: "I just stopped dead. It came to me, completely surrounded me, and I got icy cold—just freezing! And all of a sudden I felt very comfortable with it and I realized it was not there to cause problems. I just happened to be there at the right time in the right spot to where it was going to interact. Then it just backed off and vanished."

Kent describes his sensation as being "a very strange feeling." He has a theory: "I am a firm believer that there's much in this world that we can't explain. To say that *we* are the only level of lifeform is ludicrous. I've done some infrared photography and it shows me a lot that's not there. It picks up body heat—your mark, your trail."

Kent shows me samples of his work—mainly hand-painted black and white photography. But there are some beautiful women in his photographic collection. Also some oil rigs in the gulf, with the setting sun as the backdrop. And his experimental works: infrared photographs and superimposed forms.

When we go back to the subject of strange things, Kent points out that most of the activities seem to occur in the month of August. He wonders aloud if this date might coincide with the death of some previous occupant. Or perhaps it dates back to New Iberia's outlaw days and the poor fellow unearthed beneath the showroom floor.

The interior of this old building, with its high ceilings and tall walls, and the echoing footsteps as we walk across battered, hardwood floors, is the perfect setting for eerie encounters. Perhaps that explains what happens to me when I finally go into the darkroom.

I am surrounded by blackness as I wind my way amid the partitions that Kent has set up to keep out the light. Presently, I am standing in the exact spot where Kent encountered the "entity" that night in the doorway. While Kent is telling me about that incident, I sense the strangeness that he must have felt, and absent-mindedly rub at the chill in my left arm.

Noticing this, Kent pauses and says, "Yeah, he's here. I have the same goose bumps you do.... He's here."

YANKEE HEADQUARTERS STILL?

Ile Carencro, the pre-Civil War home of David and Lucinda Edmonds, is disarmingly tranquil. Located on the edge of Buzzards' Prairie near Sunset, this early Acadian plantation house (circa 1790) sits quietly beneath a grove of stately oak and pecan trees. But it was not always so peaceful. During the Civil War it was filled with the cries of wounded and dying men, while surgeons went about their bloody work, and battle raged all around, and the mistress of the house, a pregnant lady named Constance Guidry, played the piano and sang to the dying soldiers.

Is Constance still in the house, perhaps looking after children instead of wounded men? And what about the soldiers who sometimes come in the night? Or the humming voices and dancing spheres of light?

Certainly the blood stains are still there. So are the double, strap-hinged doors that were used as stretchers and operating tables. There's also a few army lanterns, a bullet hole or two, cannon balls, and burn marks on the floor. But the grimmest reminder is the bullet with the teethmarks. Looking at it now, even after all these years, the phrase "bite the bullet" takes on a special poignancy, and one can almost see the poor soldier clamping down on it, hear his muffled cries, sense the pain.

But just getting to Ile Carencro is a heady experience: three-quarters of a mile of dusty winding lane through a lush, cultivated field; a feeling that the road leads nowhere. Then a clump of trees, a shaded drive, and, finally, an ancient house with a high-pitched roof looming out of the surrounding foliage like an enormous white giant. The old Vermilionville-Opelousas Stagecoach Road, which it once faced, is long gone, but a distant line of trees mark the site of the old crossing over Bayou Carencro.

As I step through the doorway from a large front gallery, I have an overwhelming sensation that I have stepped back in time.

Yes, Ile Carencro is a haunted house.

Presently, I am seated on an antique red sofa in a dimly lit room beneath exposed wooden beams. In spite of the age of this house—or perhaps because of it—there is an ambience of ease and comfort, with an old fireplace and cypress wood smell.

The permanent wooden crosses on the walls, I am told, were placed there by Lucinda's ancestors shortly after the war, mainly because of all the soldiers who had died in these two front rooms, and in the belief that it would ward away the spirits.

Dr. David Edmonds, an economics professor at the University of Southwestern Louisiana, tells me again (the first time he told me was when I was his student several years ago) that he became interested in the history of this house when he and his wife inherited it in the early 1970's. In his research he discovered enough material to put together a lengthy book (*Yankee Autumn in Acadiana*) about the Great Texas Overland Expedition, which culminated in disaster for the Union invaders only a couple of miles up the road. David was so enthralled with his work that he stayed with it for years, even when he was a visiting Fulbright professor in Mexico, and when "things" started happening in the house.

Not that strange happenings are new at Ile Carencro. Long before the Edmonds' moved in, there were reports of flashing lights, of automobiles and tractors that would start by themselves, and of shaking ground and strange noises. Not to mention the little man in the bowler hat that sometimes knocked on the front door in broad daylight (only to disappear when the door was opened) or the sounds of a lady singing in the night.

David took no heed of the old Cajun living up the road who told him, "I wouldn't live in that house for a million dollars." Another man advised him to tear the place down and use the cypress for a more modern house. And the painter who helped with the restoration, though he was under indictment for his second manslaughter, was afraid to enter the house alone.

David says he dismissed all these tales as "so much superstitious drivel" until the night that Christopher, who was two or three at the time, came charging into the living room all wide-eyed and breathless with excitement. "Mama, Mama," he announced, pointing toward an adjoining room, "there's a man in there!"

Both David and Lucinda inspected the room carefully, and found nothing but silence. Then they searched the rest of the house, all the time questioning Chris, who was still frightened and excited. Yes, the child insisted, he had definitely seen a man in that room, and, no, he hadn't imagined it. He said the stranger was bearded, that he was wearing dark clothing with shiny buttons, and that he had picked himself off the floor and rushed into a corner. Chris also indicated that the man seemed to be clutching at his throat, which was gushing blood.

One of the curiosities about this incident was that it occurred while the crosses were off the walls. David was doing restoration work at the time and had taken them down in order to repair the old mud-and-moss (boussilage) walls beneath.

The Edmonds' did not sleep well that night. But the really intriguing revelation came a couple of weeks later, when David was examining the diary of a Union surgeon who had ministered to the wounded and dying at Ile Carencro. "There it was," says David, his gray eyes sparkling, "almost exactly as Chris described it."

David stands up, stretches his lengthy frame, and goes into the little side room that serves as his office. A couple of minutes later he emerges with several well-worn documents in his hand, one of which is labeled "Diary of Surgeon James B. Hunter, 60th Indiana Infantry."

I read about the ambulance loads of wounded and dying pouring into the house, about the grisly operations, the amputations and suffering while bales of cotton are scattered about the floor for the wounded to lie on, and limbs and bodies are piled on the front porch. There is a surgeon with the unlikely but appropriate name of Slaughter involved in this business, and through it all, the thundering guns of the Chicago Mercantile and 17th Ohio Batteries keep the attacking Texans at bay.

Then I come to the part about the "delirious soldier in the next room," who, the diary says, "plunged his pocket knife into his neck...which severed the vertebral artery and lacerated the thyroid plexus." In his dying moments, the poor boy stood up and dashed across the room, with *blood gushing from his neck.*

While David, in his sedate manner, is reluctant to discuss his experiences, Lucinda, a computer systems' analyst, doesn't seem to mind at all. A petite lady with hazel eyes, light brown hair and a casual demeanor, she tells me about the time when they had just moved here from Washington, D.C., and their daughter Julie was only two-and-a-half months old: "I had put the baby down on a quilt in the nursery near the kitchen while I was cleaning the dishes. Then I heard someone laughing...grown people...like a man and woman."

Thinking perhaps her mother and father had come by for a visit, and gone into Julie's room from the other entrance, she decided to join them. But when she went in, she found that Julie was quite alone.

Even more mysterious was the fact that the child had been moved across the room and placed near a stack of toys: "At that age, she could not possibly have crawled there by herself, and yet, she was there, smiling and giggling and having a wonderful time, just as though someone was playing with her."

Lucinda says the house was locked, "and we were alone." She also notes that the incident occurred during the period of restoration, when the crosses were off the wall.

A few years later, when their son, Alex, was about a year old, Lucinda heard the sound of humming from his room: "It wasn't Alex, because it was a grown woman's voice, and very beautiful. Again I wondered if my mother or sister or one of my aunts had come in without me seeing them, so I went in to check. No one was there except Alex."

But Lucinda was horrified to notice that the crib railing had fallen open, creating a dangerous situation. Yet the child was on the other side, seemingly mesmerized and out of harm's way. She feels certain that Alex was saved from injury that day by the humming, and that someone or something was trying to alert her while occupying the baby's attention.

And does she have any idea who or what?

"Well, I'm not ready to commit myself, but if such things do exist then I'd like to think it was one of my ancestors, since so many of them have lived—and died—in this house over the years."

She also wonders if the apparition she saw in

the living room one night, near the location of the piano, was Constance Guidry, her great-great aunt, who sang for the dying soldiers. It was late, the house was dark, and there was no moon: "Yet there she was, a white woman with black, almond-shaped eyes and a long, antebellum dress. She was standing in the doorway with her hands down at her sides."

Was she a solid figure, like a live person?

"Not exactly. She seemed to be made up of a vaporous white substance, like the fade-out in the old *Star Trek* television series when a character is beamed to another location."

Lucinda is a gifted and natural artist. Perhaps that explains why she is so sensitive to such things. Like the night she was awakened by the feeling of a presence at her bedside, as though a "terribly distressed" person was standing there wringing its hands and asking, "Why am I here?" She says the feeling communicated to her was one of "utter despair," and it took days for her to get over it.

Or the night she sensed the presence of a soldier in the living room, near a cold spot, while entertaining an unannounced visitor who claimed to possess psychic powers: "I had the distinct impression that the soldier was very young—about sixteen or seventeen—and small. I was about to ask the psychic if he felt it too, but before I could say anything, he told me all about it, and his description matched mine exactly."

Lucinda is not the only one to encounter strange things. Last April, on the date coinciding with the first Yankee occupation of the house, Julie (who is now seventeen and a student at

USL), came out of a back room where she was watching television and practically walked into a lady standing in a nearby doorway. It was midnight, and Julie and a girlfriend hastily retreated back into the den and locked themselves in for the night. Julie's description of the lady is almost exactly the same as Lucinda's, even down to the style of dress, location, and substance.

Julie has had other experiences, including a brief visit on the night of her 16th birthday from a young Union soldier. But, like her father, she doesn't like to talk about it. She says only that he was small and unshaven, that he wore a cap and uniform, and stood at the foot of her bed for a moment before disappearing. When pressed, she also admits he came to visit her in her room on an earlier occasion, while small spheres of light seemed to be dancing about.

Did it frighten her?

"It did the first time. I was really scared, and ran downstairs."

What about now? Is she afraid to sleep in the room alone?

"Not anymore," she replies. Like her mother she doesn't think he means her any harm, and the only unkind thing he's ever done was to send her a message that he thought some of her clothes "looked kind of silly."

We go upstairs to have a look at her room. It is the same room that Constance slept in while the Yankees were occupying her home. Aside from the wide-planked cypress boards, the antique iron bed and the chair-railing, it could be just another teenage girl's room. David pulls back a small throw rug and shows me an area of charred floor.

"Damn Yankees!" he says, feigning indignation.

David explains that during the first Union invasion in April of 1863 (the second invasion was in autumn of the same year) four Yankee generals, including General Banks, had commandeered the house, it being a convenient campsite alongside Bayou Carencro. During that time they banished Constance, who was seven-months' pregnant, to the upper rooms, but otherwise treated her with respect. On their departure, however, the house and grounds were occupied by drunken, rowdy soldiers who overturned a pot of burning coals on the floor and caused a small fire.

Lucinda asks David to tell about the time he solved an old murder mystery. It takes a while, not so much because David speaks slowly—he is originally from Mississippi—as because of his reluctance to admit anything out of the ordinary.

It seems that in November of 1863, just a day or two before the Battle of Bayou Bourbeux, a Union captain by the name of Jeremiah Gue, 24th Iowa, was gunned down near the front doorsteps of Ile Carencro by a group of soldiers dressed in Yankee uniforms: "This happened in broad daylight, well inside the Union camp, and in the presence of many witnesses. The killers stripped Gue's body down to his drawers, took his clothing, sword, pistol, boots and even a watch, then mounted up and rode off."

Not until the killers were safely away did the stunned onlookers realize that Gue had been killed by Confederates dressed as Yankees. "This really upset them," says David, "the idea that guerrillas could come right into their camp. So they arrested a few ignorant old men in the vicinity and tried to beat a confession out of them. When that didn't work, they stole all their livestock, ransacked their houses, and burned some barns and houses. They never did learn who the killers were, but in their letters and diaries they talked about it for weeks. And always the unanswered question: who killed Jeremiah Gue?

David wondered too, so much so that he began to dream about the incident. Then one day, tired from his writing, he dozed off in his study—and suddenly found himself surrounded by Yankees in uniform, including one Jeremiah Gue.

Captain Gue, speaking in his farm boy Iowa accent, said how pleased he was with David's work: "Another Yankee chimed in, and before long they were all telling me how grateful they were that someone was finally telling their story, saying that perhaps now they could rest. They also offered to help, saying they could clarify details about this and that, and telling me where to look for verification."

So David asked Captain Gue to name his assassins and to give the reason: "Captain Gue answered that the people in the vicinity had suffered so much from the invasion that a band of local Confederates—as opposed to the Texans—had decided to do something spectacular. This was supposed to raise their spirits...and to demoralize the invaders. As to the identity of his killers, he said the information would be forthcoming within a day or two, and that it would come from Baton Rouge."

After this "dream," David had the distinct notion that the answer could be found in the LSU archives: "And sure enough, the very next day a colleague from the USL library—Carl Brasseaux—called to say that he'd recently seen a document at LSU that might be of interest to me."

David went there immediately and examined the wartime diary of a lady from Abbeville (Priscilla Bond). "Incredibly, it was all there, just as Jeremiah Gue had said, including the name of the man who had pulled the trigger, Pete Aleman."

Not all spirits seemed pleased with David's work—or perhaps the lack of it. One night before he finished his book, he was abruptly awakened by a slap on the face! He says the incident could be attributed to a beetle flying, "or something." But he also points out that it occurred at a time when he was getting slack in his work, and he jokingly wonders if his Yankee friends weren't telling him to get moving.

On the other hand, there's no accounting for the noises that the Edmonds' keep hearing in the downstairs front room, the same room where Constance played the piano for the dying soldiers, and the room where Chris encountered the apparition. Sometimes it sounds like furniture being moved; at other times like something soft being dragged across the floor. "Like a dead body," suggests David, a bit uneasily.

Then there's the story of the singing and piano playing, which neighbors, previous residents and tenants swear they have heard over the years. David scoffs at the idea, pointing out that there's a lounge nearby, and when the wind is right you can hear the music.

But that doesn't explain what the old lady in Grand Coteau told a television crew from "That's Incredible." Her father was a slave on the place, and she lived there with him until his death about 1920. In her nineties and very frail, she wrinkled her weathered nose when she spoke, and her hands and voice trembled: "Oh, she's there, all right...that old lady who'd sing for de Yankees. I done heard her. Lots o' times...."

MARSHMALLOW

A suicide pact resulting in the deaths of two brothers seems to be having its strange effects in a mobile home near Grand Coteau. Or perhaps it's because the trailer is situated atop a burial ground for slaves. And then there's the theory that buried treasure may have something to do with all the goings-on. Not to mention the slave who was said to be interred with the booty to protect it! Or the tragedies that have occurred at Dead Man's Curve on the road outside. Finally, there is a character named Marshmallow—at least in the mind of a three-year-old—who seems to bring the pieces together.

The story takes place off Louisiana Highway 182, just across a long sweeping curve from a stately plantation home still surrounded by moss-draped live oaks. I arrive there with a friend shortly before nightfall, and am met at the door by Tim Guilbeau. He lives there with his wife, Dixie, a student at USL, and his young son, Brandon.

The Guilbeau family believes that their home rests over the burial ground for slaves of days-gone-by. They know that it's flanked by the homes of Tim's uncles, both of whom shot themselves to death with the same shotgun, one five years ago, the other twenty-five years ago.

The first indication that anything was awry occurred in April of 1987, during the time of the anniversary of the suicides. A framed picture flew across the room all by itself. Dixie saw it in mid-air. Shortly afterwards, while her father was in the kitchen, papers from atop the refrigerator began floating straight down to the floor in an unusual manner. Tim adds that doors slammed without prompting, objects threw themselves around, while other items simply came up missing.

"Things were falling off the walls," says Dixie, speaking in a soft tone, "and in the cabinets you could hear things shifting around. That whole day was really bizarre. We were finding things in the weirdest places."

One night that same week Dixie was awakened by the sound of her child's stuffed chime ball. She walked to the living room to find the toy spinning a circular pattern on the carpet. Brandon, her three-year-old, was in his own room. Dixie says she was so startled that she rushed into her child's bedroom and took the sleeping child with her into her own room.

Two nights before this, while Dixie was studying, she heard the crinkling of paper: "So I got up and walked to the ice box to investigate, and it stopped. I sat down again and the crinkling started again, like someone balling up papers."

Lights go off and on, and the Guilbeaus sometimes return home at night to find a light burning that they were certain was off when they left. Dixie laughs while telling this and says it's "like a little jokester."

Spoons seem to be a favorite object for this "jokester." Dixie can hardly keep one in the house. She finds them in the yard, in the oddest places in the house, or sometimes she doesn't find them at all.

Although Dixie is curious about all this, she's no stranger to the world of the extra-sensory. From the time she was very young she's had psychic experiences of one kind or another. For one thing, her dreams sometimes come true: "I woke up in a cold sweat one night. I was having a dream about a friend of mine who was in a box and couldn't get out."

Several days later she learned that on the same night as her dream her friend's car had plunged off the road and gone under water, trapping him inside. Although his lungs collapsed he survived the accident. "It's a miracle that he was saved," she says.

On another occasion she had a feeling that a different friend had been killed in a car accident, and she mentioned this to someone who knew that person. No, she was told, the friend was alive and well. But two days later the friend was dead, the victim of an automobile accident.

Dixie has also had out-of-body experiences since about the age of eighteen, all of them involuntary. At first they were frightening: "I was a freshman in college and had such an active social life that I was on the point of total mental and physical exhaustion. It would happen and I couldn't control it. Like two me's. I could feel it coming on. I'd almost have to literally drag myself to the bed.... I'd start feeling kind of numb. I'd want to move and it was like pieces of me would die, one at a time. I was...paralyzed. It was like a force pulling on me, and then I was out."

She says she could do lots of things in this state, like listening in on her parents' conversations, or even such physical things as turning on the stereo: "Later I would tell them what they said and they wondered how I knew. It was like the 'me' down there was dead, while the one floating above—the inner me—was laughing and saying 'I'm going to do this and this.' Things I touched or moved then were actually moved after."

Dixie fought it in the beginning, and the experiences were usually short-lived. She told no one at first, but then she discovered that it happens to other people, and that some of them actually worked at projecting themselves (astrally) onto another plane. Now she can stop it from coming on altogether.

Brandon seems to have inherited some of his mother's sensitivities. From the time he was about eighteen-months' old he has talked about a nonexistent lady he calls "Marshmallow." He doesn't like her and describes her as a big, mean, black lady who lives down the road and eats squirrel. Marshmallow, he says, has "blue" magic.

His mother says that when he talks to Marshmallow it's like he's in a trance. He even learned a French phrase from her. Dixie smiles and speculates that maybe "it's a slave that Brandon sees, and maybe her name is some strange African name he can't pronounce."

Brandon's room is a comfortable, colorful place with all the toys and trappings of any other three-year-old. Yet it seems to be the center of misgivings for both the child and his mother. Says Dixie: "Brandon doesn't like to go into his room alone, and when I sleep in there I have nightmares."

Perhaps the reason is on the other side of Dead Man's Curve, in an upper window of the old plantation house. Legend has it that you can look out that window—and no other—and see the exact spot where the household treasure was buried

to save it from the advancing Yankees. Some of the old timers even claim that a slave was sacrificed and buried with it to serve as guardian.

We pull back the curtain on Brandon's bedroom window and peer out at the house across the road. Darkness has fallen, and there's an occasional rumble of distant thunder, with the threat of rain. Dixie explains that this is the only window in the trailer with a direct view of the window "over there." Someone else wonders if all the slaves were buried on this same spot beneath where we are now standing. Could it be that the treasure, too, is buried here? And Marshmallow?

NIGHT CALLER

Just when it seems that tales of apparitions and other unearthly happenings are falling into a neat, discernible pattern, another kind of story emerges, this one shattering the myth that "haunted" places have a history of tragic circumstances.

Julie Comeaux's house in Broussard is situated in a quiet residential neighborhood on a tree-lined street. It does not have a tragic past. In fact, it is of fairly recent construction. And yet Julie (not her real name) was visited one night by the grandmother who had raised her, the same grandmother who had died in a nursing home a month earlier.

Although it occurred fifteen years ago (when Julie was about twenty), Julie says it seems like yesterday: "I was in bed sleeping when all of a sudden I heard the doorbell ring. I knew it was the front doorbell because it rings twice. No one ever uses the front door at my house. I tried to wake my husband, but he sleeps so soundly, I couldn't. I'm afraid of the dark, but I got up anyway. I turned on the light in the entry hall and then on the porch, and looked through the peep hole."

Julie gets emotional and seems to fight back tears in her brown eyes as she remembers: "I opened the door and there she was. Beautiful! Beautiful! Even though I knew she had died I wasn't frightened.... I said, 'Mom!' and immediately went to hug her. But I couldn't touch her.

My arms were there, but I couldn't touch her."

The visitor never spoke: "She had a haze around her, a light. She looked at me, and all I did was look at her. And then she turned her head and looked at the road. There was a car.... I have never in my life seen a car like that! It was, long, long, long! It was black and there was a man standing at the door of the car. She turned and looked back at me.... It was time for her to go."

Julie and her grandmother were very close, and Julie visited her often in the nursing home. During those visits, Mom, as Julie called her, would often remark in French—she spoke no English—"I'd love to go see your new home, Julie." But she was too weak and sick to move, and died without fulfilling her wish.

Apparently she fulfilled her desire that night. Julie says that although her grandmother had suffered for years, she looked healthy and radiant when she came calling; younger, too. She seemed her age, yet beautiful.

"I knew she was dead, but for some strange reason I accepted the fact that she was at the door. I wasn't scared. Nothing went through my mind. I was satisfied just looking at her. I hadn't been able to go up to the coffin to look at her."

This was not Julie's first encounter with the supernatural. When she was seven she had an unusual "dream" that she believes was inspired by her sad state of affairs. Her mother had recently abandoned her and her sister, and her father had to join the service to provide for them. Although her grandmother had taken them in, Julie just wasn't herself, and seemed to withdraw from everything, even to the extent of not talking.

"I was disgusted with the situation," says Julie. "They'd take me to the doctor. They didn't know what was wrong. I knew what was wrong: I wanted my mother. I wanted my father. Couldn't have 'em, so I gave up on everything." Julie recalls that she was a very ill child living in poverty.

Her grandmother took her to Mass every day at the Cathedral in Lafayette. One day she asked a priest to pray for Julie. The priest told her that he was going to pray to Saint Theresa, and then he prayed while Julie knelt before him.

Afterwards, Julie "dreamed" she was on her front porch sitting in the lap of a small woman. The woman was wearing "this long, light blue dress, and she looked like what I thought the Blessed Mother would look like. She was very young and beautiful."

The lady had a rosary wrapped around her waist, and it hung all the way to the floor: "I never saw a long rosary like that. All around the porch was this haze—a bright, bright light. I couldn't see anything past the haze except the roses. There were roses everywhere. Big, beautiful roses. Other than the light, all I could see were the roses and this beautiful little face. Evidently all night long I sat on her lap. She never spoke a word to me. But I never in my life had such peace. I can't explain it."

Julie was awakened the next morning by her grandmother, who was shaking her violently and crying: "She thought I was dead. I wouldn't move. I was straight, stiff and ice cold. Evidently I didn't want to wake up. You have to understand: I was seven, and all my life I had nothing but trouble. And this was the most peaceful thing I'd ever experienced. When I woke up I felt great. I never had trouble again. Now, that was *not* just a dream!"

Julie has had other extra-sensory experiences, most of them in the form of dreams and premonitions. Her mother also experiences these. And her grandmother was a *traiteur*, a healer of sunstroke. Perhaps the sensitivity is hereditary.

Yet, for all that, the night visit of Julie's grandmother and the dream she had as a seven-year-old were by far the most important, "because they weren't normal, everyday things. Now I get chills, and I get emotional when I think about it."

Julie looks around a moment, smiles, and concludes with another thought: "These scientists and educated people want you to believe these things can't happen. But when these things happen to you, you know for sure there has to be life after death."

SARAH'S CURSE

Sarah Plantation was little more than a cane field in the 1970's. And it was long ago when Sarah cursed the bank for taking the land away from her. But those who live in the Iberia Parish area of Morbihan know well the declaration Sarah made—that anyone who lived on her land in the future would come to grief.

But Allen Babineaux, a fireman by profession, didn't believe in such nonsense. Neither did Anne, his cheerful, green-eyed wife. So they bought a lot on Sarah Plantation. Then they bought a two-and-a-half story house in New Iberia that had to be moved to make room for a parking lot. This they dismantled—it was too large to be moved

otherwise—and moved to their new property on Sarah Plantation, where they put it back together. Standing alone amid fields of swaying sugar cane, their's was the very first house in the new residential development.

The Babineaux's and their five children then set about the task of restoring the old house. At first everything seemed to be going along fine, but then something happened to make them think about Sarah's curse.

"The clock was the first instance," says Anne, speaking to me from the sofa in her living room. "It'd be on twelve o'clock one minute, then you'd come back downstairs and it'd be one o'clock." It was as though the clock refused to accept Daylight Savings Time; otherwise, it worked just fine.

She also tells me about the footsteps on the old wooden stairs, saying the children were the only ones at first to hear the sounds: "They were terrified. Then one morning when Allen and I lay in bed late, we heard this heavy 'flop, flop, flop' coming up the stairs. I leaned over the railing to look, but there was no one there."

One day when Anne was alone in the house and painting the girls' second floor bathroom, the downstairs portable TV came on at full volume. She had just been down there for a coffee break and was certain she had turned it off, but now it was "blasting away" as though some invisible hand was at work. Anne readily confesses that the experience shook her feelings of security.

There were more such disturbances in the following days and months. Radios would turn off and on by themselves; lights would flash on, sometimes startling the children. Or, in an unusual twist, the lights would sometimes startle the invisible presence, as when Jena, then aged eleven, was yelled at for switching on a light in the bathroom. "Turn it off!" shouted a woman's voice, though no one was apparently around. Anne says Jena turned "white as the stove" and dashed out of the bathroom.

And then there was the night of the storm: "The windows have these old weights in them," explains Anne, "and they're very hard to raise. During the rain storm all of the windows in Jami's room suddenly flew up at the same time. Jami, who was fifteen-years-old, came down the stairs four at time!"

Before long, the children began to ask what was going on, and Anne, not wanting them to be frightened, kept explaining away all the strange happenings as having a logical explanation: "I knew I couldn't tell them what I think is here...what I know is here."

Though most of the incidents were frightening, sometimes they were just plain aggravating, as in the case of the disappearing oysters: "I was going to try a new recipe of oyster dressing for Christmas dinner. I hid the oysters in the refrigerator and planned to sneak them into the dressing. The next morning the jar of oysters and a sixteen-slice package of cheese were gone."

Since no one in the family eats raw oysters, and since no one had any strong reasons for objecting to her proposed concoction, the disappearance—like all the other happenings—remains a mystery.

Anne says she has lived in fourteen different houses since she was fourteen-years-old, but "This is the first time I have ever experienced a feeling that someone is watching." She says all of the family—and visitors—have expressed more or less the same feeling, especially in the master bedroom and bath. Anne describes the sensation as a "thick" or "heavy" feeling of a presence. She adds that some members of the family will not even go into this bathroom after sunset because of the terrible feeling that comes over them.

Other things have happened at the house, even apparitions, as when Anne's then seven-year-old son, Frank, claimed to have seen a small boy dressed in silver-colored, short pants standing in the front doorway. On another occasion he saw a uniformed soldier wearing a brown cap at the foot of his bed.

Anne forbade her children to mention these occurrences at school out of concern that other parents would not allow their children to visit. For the Babineauxs, who enjoy the presence of children—even to the extent of opening their home to foreign exchange students—it would be tragic. In any case, friends of the children seemed to sense that something was not right without being told, often exclaiming that the house felt "creepy."

Not that it kept them away. For example, some of Joni's friends stopped by one night to pick up some cassette tapes. Since no one but Joni was home they asked if they could have a look around. All well and good until they walked into the guest bedroom and found a man standing behind the door. The girls fled from the house in terror. So stunned were they that it wasn't until they'd driven to New Iberia that they were able to talk about their experience.

By this time Allen had had enough! One day he phoned Anne from the fire station to tell her about an article he had just read in *Reader's Digest*. It seems that a family on the Hudson River was having the same experiences while restoring an old house. This gave him an idea. "I'm going to get rid of it," he told her in no uncertain terms.

Later that day he went into the bathroom where the presence was usually the strongest. There was no question that it was there. Though Allen is a big man, well equipped to deal with physical problems, this was something different. Still, he had made up his mind. "Go away and leave us alone!" he commanded. "We did not tear down this house. We're restoring it. Whoever you are, go away, now!"

Apparently it did, and Anne says there's been no trouble since. "I'm glad its gone," she says. But then she looks around and adds, "I'd love to know who it was. I think often of Sarah's curse."

'T-FRERE'S AMELIE

Peggy Moseley is the mistress of 'T-Frere's, an elegant bed-and-breakfast inn on Highway 339 in Lafayette. She lives there with her husband, an engineer. She is also a teacher of the blind. After talking with her I could not help but wonder if we are not all "blind" in some ways.

My interview with her took place on a stormy February evening in a cozy corner of her kitchen seated before a warm fireplace. As lightning flashed and thunder rumbled through the night, Mrs. Moseley spoke softly of the spiritual presence in her home, an entity she calls "Amelie." But let's allow this lovely lady to tell her story in her own eloquent words.

Most of us tend to deny our extra-sensory experiences. But there's another world right across—waiting to be recognized, to be explored, and to instruct!

We've had many things happen here. A Cambridge professor tried to tell my husband—

who is an engineer—that he needs to be open to all experiences. When we close ourselves off, we close ourselves off to other avenues of information. My husband lives in the sensory world where for everything there is cause and effect.

Our house was built about 1890 by Oneziphore Comeaux. They called him T-Frere because he was the youngest of seven children. We call it T-Frere's House. It's built all of cypress. It has been changed somewhat and gentrified, made more lovely and elegant with 20th century materials, but it still lives well. We've lived here since 1975.

I certainly never dreamed that there was something that moved about. My first experience happened one afternoon. It was about three o'clock and all my lingerie which had been downstairs in the bachelor's chest was folded neatly on the bed upstairs. It had been moved, and I thought "What a strange, peculiar thing for the housekeeper to do!" It wasn't at all like Louella to do that sort of thing, so I took my things back down to the cabinet in the girls' room. But the next afternoon, the same thing happened again.

On the third day I asked Louella, "Why do you move my lingerie?"

She said, "I didn't move it and I'm going to tell you something: I'm not here by myself. I see things moving and I tell you what else: I'm going to quit."

I said, "Oh, that's silly...you can't quit."

She said, "I'm terrified to stay here. There are things that move around. I see lights. I see shadows. And I don't like it here!"

Two weeks later while I was talking on the phone to my friend, Patricia, I heard a tremendous crashing and banging in the pantry. I started screaming for my son, Matthew. I thought he was the culprit. I went back to the pantry and everything was off the shelves. Everything smashed, broken...as though a tornado hit it. Matthew came running from the barn, so it wasn't he. Pat got in her car, came over immediately, and helped pick up the mess.

At that time I realized that possibly there was something outside the sensory world and I felt it—at that point—to be evil, malicious, and malevolent. I asked a friend who speaks French, Stephen Coussan, to come over to tell her that "In God's name I'm going to burn this house down if you misbehave to this extent!"

I felt it to be female and that it was important to communicate in French. I said, "Tell her she is to leave my children alone! And she is to leave me alone, and if she wishes to continue living here, these are the house rules." I was very emotional because of the mess she had made. I felt I was dealing with something very capricious and angry. I was angry enough not to be frightened.

That was the last incident we had of breakage and destruction. I felt that she resented the fact that I was neither French nor Catholic. When we played hymns on the piano, if the candles were lit, the wax would go all over although there was no draft. And I thought, "I don't believe she likes Protestant hymns."

An old black neighbor asked me, "Have you met her? There is someone there. She walks." He told me about a woman who had lived here and who had been very unhappy and who died here, childless and alone—when she was thirty-two years old. And by accident. This may be the same person.

My mother, who is a Southern Baptist and not given to believing in ghosts, came and asked, "Who is the little Cajun lady that comes and talks to me? When I'm out working in the back [planting bulbs] there's a little lady; she wears her hair parted down the center, she wears it back in a bun."

My mother described her dress as an ashes of roses [color], and said that she had a cleft in her chin and spoke only French. My mother also said, "She's kind of old-fashioned. I just wish she could speak English because she's so nice."

I made a point then to go up and down the street asking old neighbors to tell me who is petite, speaks no English, comes and goes, and wears ashes of roses. No one could name the person.

The petite one also came to our daughter Mary's wedding. Mary was married here at the house. We had invited about two-hundred people. Mother had brought a lot of food because we were catering it ourselves. We had made golden yellow punch. But I noticed during the reception that the punch was chartreuse. It was the ugliest shade of green.... This is bizarre.

After the wedding was over and all of the relatives and guests had gone, I said, "Mother, what happened to the punch? Why was it chartreuse?"

She said, "It was the Cajun lady. She was out there in the kitchen, over in the corner. She poured green food coloring into the punch and I said, Stop! Stop!" Mother wanted to know who the woman was.

If I had told my mother, "What I think you saw may not have been from our time," she'd have had me committed. The punch was dreadful, and the culprit was the little Cajun lady.

I believe her to be "Amelie" who lived here at one time. According to diaries and legend, she drowned in the cistern. She had a fever. She apparently had gone to cool off behind the house.

There was a Steinway piano in the hall at one time. I was coming down the staircase about three o'clock in the afternoon. We get a lot of sunshine coming through the front door. It was an ordinary, normal Saturday afternoon. Somebody, something, started at the treble end and went all the way down the keyboard. And I thought, "What the hell was that?" And I ran outside. I got very excited. I said, "Charlie, something ran down the keyboard!" I mean I could see the keys, I watched it go down. I'm the only one who saw it.

Charlie said, "Probably just the cat."

But we don't have a cat, so I went back into the house and I said, "You can play the piano all you want when I'm not here! And when my children are not here! But by God, you will not frighten me again this way, nor my children!"

From that day forward I would always turn the cover back so that the keys were always exposed so that if she needed to play, she could play, but not while I'm in the house. Never!

After a newspaper article about the house came out—a feature by Mario Mamalakis in the *Daily Advertiser*—I got about three telephone calls. Each person wanted to establish credibility. They'd say, "I do this," or "I do that," or "This is my occupation."

One lady came as a visitor—she was waiting for Suzanne Olivier, a previous tenant—and was about to come in when she saw a rocking chair with a woman sitting in it...only she could see the light coming through her. When she realized what was happening she was so terrified that she ran to her car.

Another caller said, "Don't ever watch Johnny Carson by yourself." She said when she stayed here once she was watching Johnny Carson and she was laughing. She realized someone was in the room laughing with her. She was terrified.

Suzanne said that an imperceptible someone had thrown bread across the room, and then knocked a collection of vases off the kitchen window and broken them.

These things are frightening. And other people have had experiences here. We had a renter, an anesthesiologist from Lake Charles, who called Charlie and said, "There's someone in your house. You'd better get home because I believe there's a burglary in progress."

He had come to bring his rent check, and was walking, looking at the height and architecture of the house when he saw someone looking down at him from the upstairs window.

Charlie came and checked the house, but it was just as we had left it, except that the upstairs drapery was closed. They're always left open just as they are right now.

So I called the gentleman that night, and he said, "Mrs. Moseley, I'm just reporting what I saw. And I saw someone in your house. And she was looking down at me. And she would not answer the door. Mrs. Moseley, I'm telling you, somebody was in your house, and I saw her and she saw me and pulled the curtain closed."

A friend, who is a world-renowned botanist, was driving down the road with his wife at midnight. I believe the year was 1978. They described a brilliant green light from above over this house and property. He said it was very beautiful. I begged him to give me some meaning. "What was it?" I asked.

He said, "I have no idea. I only report what I saw."

A French engineer who speaks three languages stayed here. At breakfast he described the little lights that came up through the floor and down the hall and on the front gallery. Charles explained to this knowledgeable scientist the refractive properties of light. This Frenchman said, "No, no, when I put my foot on them, they not come on top of my shoe."

Both he and his wife saw it. This person was a scientist, accustomed to order, cause and effect.

The date was August fifteenth of last year. It was the Harmonic Progression—from the old Mayan calendar when the planets are lined up and the world becomes harmonic. I did not know.

This may or may not have to do with the ghost that we know, or the energy that comes and goes. But it is my personal belief that just as there are places of longitude—for example, you know you can cross the equator and never see it—that there may be psychic points of intersection where things are accelerated or where, if Einstein is correct, the past and the future can bleed through to those who are accepting, or tuned-in. It occurs to me more and more that this house may be a point of psychic intersection.

As for Amelie, I have seen her. She woke me up. I was fast asleep on the couch and I woke up with my arm being suspended and I was being pulled and I looked up and saw her. The light seemed to be coming from behind her. My house was filled with smoke. She literally pulled me to my feet. She was pleading. There was a lot of light; I jumped up and went tearing through to the kitchen and opened the dishwasher. A wooden spoon had lodged and the whole end had been completely charred. There was no danger of fire, but the house was filled with smoke. It was at that point I knew absolutely that I was not dealing with an enemy.

Several years ago I had the flu. I was upstairs shivering and hurting. No one was here, and I thought I was going to die. I was unable to get up and go downstairs for my goose-down comforter.

Much later I woke up and the goose-down comforter that I had wanted was over me. I was finally warm. I felt very wonderful and I said mentally, "I thank you very much; you're very kind!" That was my first instinct—to say, "Thank you."

And I'm sure if I said this in front of Charlie, he'd say, "You had fever, you were aching; you have no recall. There's a reason."

I think there probably is a reason. And I give it to you. I think this house sits at a point of psychic intersection. Just like I turn on my old 1932 radio. I can't tell you how it happens, it just does.

My son Matthew could not pass geometry in high school. He needed a "B" on his final exam and he studied and studied, but finally was resigned that he couldn't learn in one night what had eluded him all year. He went to bed. The next morning he got up and said, "I'm going to ace the exam. I dreamt last night about this little lady. She came and she taught me. She had a chalkboard in my room."

I said, "Describe her."

"Well," he said, "she was tiny; she had her hair pulled back. She was kind of old-fashioned but she was a wonderful teacher. Nobody ever explained it to me so that I could understand it."

What really happened? What difference does it make? He made the "B" he needed.

I have not seen her lately. If she came today, I would tell her the day and the year and the name of the President of the United States. I would try to give her a point of reference. And that's what I'd want someone to do for me if I were lost. I would quietly tell her, "You're in the wrong time. You've slipped across. This is my time. Your time is somewhere else. God's love. God's peace. Godspeed."

SHOES ON THE STAIRS

Most people sit up and listen when Mike Fletcher tells them he lives in a renovated chicken coop on family property. But he and his wife, Cherie, have done wonders with the old place, converting it into comfortable living quarters with a nice, down-homey atmosphere. Mike assures me that there are no ghosts here, feathered or otherwise, and nothing else that goes bump in the night. Such was not the case with his childhood home.

Mike was born in his grandparents' home in Franklin, in an all-cypress, Acadian-style house "on the wrong side of the tracks." The house is gone now, but a huge tree with branches that used to scrape the old tin roof still stands guard at the site.

When Mike's grandfather was growing old and needed care, his children—Mike's parents—moved in with him. There were strange noises in the house even before Mike came along, and whispers that something was amiss.

Rumor had it that a beautiful young girl had once lived here, and had borne a child out-of-wedlock. Because of the shame she had brought upon her family, she and her infant child were forced to remain in the attic rooms of the house, never to be seen in public. But the strain was too much... The young mother killed her child and then took her own life.

This tragic ending seems to be the beginning of the story for the Fletcher family.

Almost every night after they went to bed, they would hear footsteps on the staircase. Mike's Dad always said it sounded like a little girl with new shoes playing on the stairs.

Mike, a physical therapy student now in his twenties, remembers it vividly. His face takes on an intense expression as he talks about his childhood experiences of trying to sleep in his bedroom—alone—when he'd hear the noises: "It sounded like she'd walk down the stairs slowly, then...slide and shuffle her feet before running back up the stairs to repeat the sequence." Mike says he was so frightened by the noise that he couldn't even scream. Instead he'd rush into his parents' bedroom.

Once, when he was twelve or thirteen, he noticed the bedroom door was ajar just enough for him to see the staircase from his bed. Hearing footsteps, he buried himself beneath the covers. After a while, however, he overcame his fear long enough to risk a look. Stripping back the covers, he felt certain that he was about to see the mysterious girl playing on the stairs. But there was nothing—no girl, no footsteps, and no noise. Nothing but silence.

Mike's father was never afraid of the little ghost. Indeed, he was rather interested in coming to know it better. Sometimes Mike would awake to find him standing at the foot of the staircase calling to the girl to come out and be seen.

A discovery in the attic seems to support the family's suspicions that the house was haunted by the spirit of a young girl. The attic was rambling, difficult to reach, and divided into many sections. One area could be entered only by removing a plywood wall and climbing through a small hole.

Exploring this hidden space, Mike's brother, Glen, found a pair of little girl's shoes placed side by side and right to left. So old were they that when he touched them they started to crumble. He finally retrieved them with a newspaper, by sliding it underneath.

Mike's brother decided to keep the shoes, but bad luck followed. His children fell ill, one so badly that he had to be hospitalized, and Glen got in a wreck in his truck, all in the same week he possessed the shoes. Glen got rid of them.

There were other inexplicable happenings in the house about this time. A clock with a broken pendulum suddenly began to chime; smoke filled the house, though nothing was afire; the cries of a baby came from the attic; and Mike's sister remembers the horrible feeling of a hand on her chest holding her down as she slept.

The disturbances got worse. For three nights in a row at exactly 2:45 a.m. things began to happen. First a shelf came loose from the wall and fell to the floor; then it was a gun rack; and then another structure.

Perhaps certain places and people are more receptive to the spiritual world than others. After Mike's grandfather died, Mike heard a door slam and went upstairs to investigate. At the top of the stairs, directly in front of attic doors to right and left, he hesitated a moment, wondering what kind of secrets they held. While standing there, a light bulb shattered directly over his head.

Could it have been caused by an electrical short? At first Mike didn't know. But several years later, he heard a curious story from his brother Glen, who knew nothing of the light bulb incident. It seems that shortly before their grandfather's death, the old man had said that if he could come back to communicate, he'd break a light bulb as a sign....

After the death of Mike's parents, the old house was torn down and its secrets destroyed. Mike smiles as he remembers: "A lot of people find it hard to believe that we heard ghosts in that house. But I guess until you hear it yourself, you can't believe it."

THE GHOST OF GRAND PRAIRIE

The owner of an historical south Louisiana home near the town of Washington inadvertently disturbs the grave of a long-deceased Canadian. He returns the favor by disturbing her peace of mind. A psychic has to be called in to mediate.

I had heard of these bizarre happenings for weeks, and from several sources. Thus it is with a great deal of excitement and anticipation that I set off to visit the site. Nell goes with me. Not only is she a friend, but she is also related to the owner of the house.

We drive down the meandering country road of Grand Prairie and take a dirt lane across acres of rolling, green pasture. Calves romp along the side of my station wagon, oblivious to clouds of dust, and I marvel at their beauty.

Finally, we pull up and stop before an ancient Acadian-style house with a tin roof and wide front gallery. A board fence, weathered and gray, surrounds the place, as do barns and other out-buildings. Everything is shaded by a pleasant grove of cedars. An elderly but spry lady is outside playing with her dog, which is jumping up on her.

The lady—who is Nell's aunt—gives us a warm welcome and tells me to call her "Maman." I learn later that she is in her eighties (86 to be precise); the house itself is two-hundred-years-old. Maman has lived here most of her life.

After hearing so many tales about this place, I'm not sure what to expect, perhaps a sense of strangeness—a meaningful chill. However, when I walk through the old entrance doors, there are no chills—not at first.

Maman confirms the story I had previously heard from Nell and another friend. But hearing it first-hand from her at the actual site is a different matter. I can smell the old cypress as she talks, hear her footsteps (and mine) echo across wide-planked flooring, and investigate the bousillage walls for myself.

The spirit in the house, we are told, first communicated its presence by means of water. Lots of it, and all unwanted. Puddles kept showing up on the floor, even when it wasn't raining. Mattresses and rugs became soaked, yet the ceiling was dry to the touch, with no sign of a leaky roof. Then everyone suspected the plumbing, but it, too passed inspection. Even when the water supply to the house was shut off, bowls somehow filled with water again and again. And Maman was often drenched by gushes from out of nowhere.

She mentions the time she was talking on the telephone to her sister when suddenly "Someone just poured a bucketful of water on my head." There were other times when she had to change clothes two or three times a night because her gown was soaked.

Family members sitting at the kitchen table are not spared either, as they must sometimes endure at least a glassful of water poured over their heads. Yet no visible source has ever been found: no glass, no bucket. Just water.

This is not a shy spirit. He'll perform his mischievous antics for visitors. When Maman first began making these reports, some of her relatives decided to stop by to check on her state of mind. They entered the house to the tune of overturning chairs. Another time, while guests were sitting on the porch, they were repeatedly bombarded and struck in the head by flying pecans—though there are no pecan trees nearby. There were also witnesses to the rain of rice that came pattering down on the tin roof one day.

Then there was the time that towels floated across the room, and sofa pillows went flying off on their own accord. Salt and pepper were mysteriously poured onto the kitchen table, and the words "hi" and "love" were found scribbled out in the mixture. The welcome mat on the front porch slammed into a car door. And gravel was thrown into the bed of a pick-up truck parked outside.

The stories are endless. A glass jar of candy went sliding along the surface of a flat table one day. Tremors shook cups and saucers on a serving tray in full view of witnesses. A heavy wooden door between the back bedroom and hallway repeatedly slammed open and shut. And pieces of China sometimes break by themselves without falling off the shelves.

One day some recipe cards spewed out all over the kitchen as in "52-card pickup." A card landed in a pot of gumbo cooking on the stove. When Maman removed it and put it into the sink, it flew out and hit her in the head, much like the dishcloth did one morning after she had washed the dishes.

Nothing is exempt from this spirit's wrath, not even religious items. A crucifix atop a dresser was thrown to the floor. Another time it went after a statue of the Madonna, cracking it for no apparent reason. Then there is the time that a holy water cup was sent spinning around the nail which affixed it to the wall. A bottle of antiseptic was mysteriously thrown, breaking a transom. And a house plant was removed from its pot indoors and placed on the front porch although the doors and the windows were closed.

The ghost gets playful at times, as he did the day he put an old cowboy hat on Maman's head. Another time he put a sheet over her head, giving *her* the appearance of a ghost! Still another time, Maman felt something cold on the back of her neck. Reaching back, she found a clothespin clipped to her collar. Her grandson also had clothespins on his collar.

Growing concerned over these episodes, and wondering just what was going on, the family decided to consult a Lake Charles woman with psychic talents. Her name is Barbara.

Even over the telephone, Barbara was able to describe the house down to incidental knick-knacks. When she inquired about renovations, Maman told her about the vinyl siding that had recently been added to the sides and back of the house, as well as the new wooden steps on the back porch. The psychic advised her that these should be removed if things were to return to normal. Maman disagreed; she hoped that all would soon be quieted down in spite of the apparently offensive additions.

But all did not quiet down, so Barbara visited the house and communicated with the spirit. Speaking to Barbara in French, it described itself as a short, overweight man from Nova Scotia with dark hair. The name was Leonce.

Barbara doesn't speak French, so she had to repeat his phrases for the tape recorder and later have it translated to understand his communications.

Leonce said he had a message for Maman: that one night many years ago when Maman's husband was alive the two of them were visited by a "peeping Tom," but he (Leonce) had scared the intruder away.

When Leonce was asked if he didn't like Maman, he replied that he did like her, and meant her no harm. The reason for his pranks, he said, was because he was disturbed by the addition of the back porch steps, which was built directly above his grave.

Maman isn't certain whether anyone is buried there or not, but she does recall that when the builders were driving a piling in that area, they had hit something which impaired their work. And Nell remembers that when she used to play there as a child, she was cautioned to stay away from the back porch area. She was told that a mother and her child had been buried there, and the children must respect the gravesite as holy ground.

Barbara also told Maman that she "saw" Civil War history at the house. She said a doctor once owned the house and had used slaves for terrible experiments. The back pasture is the burial site for these slaves, she reported.

Maman leads us into the kitchen and the three of us sit down at the table. No, she tells me, she's not afraid to live here. She even laughs as she recalls some of the pranks Leonce has played on her.

On reflection, she does admit to having been afraid once, when she distinctly heard the front door open, followed by footsteps. But, on checking, she found that she was quite alone.

Maman says that almost all of the playful activities have occurred when her grandson, Jude, is around. Jude is fifteen, and very close to Maman.

Her revelation doesn't surprise me, since most poltergeist activities seem to occur when a teenager is present. Some researchers have even hypothesized that a spirit presence can tap a teenager's energies, which (as any mother knows) is at high levels during those years.

And, indeed, something happens during the interview which causes me to believe that Jude is the key to the mystery, although he is not here at the time.

Both Nell and I have brought tape recorders and are using them as we sit talking to Maman about the ghosts in her house. About half an hour into the interview, Nell notices that her recorder has stopped taping. At first, we attribute this to weak batteries. About two minutes later, however, my recorder also stops. As I manipulate the buttons to determine the problem, it reverses and rewinds, then stops and starts recording again, only to come slowly to a strained stop, again and again.

Momentarily, the telephone rings. Maman answers, listens a few seconds, and then says, "Jude, Jude! Is that you, Jude? Who are you talking to?" Listening again, confused, she hangs up and says that he evidently couldn't hear her. He was talking to his friend, Chris, saying, "I have to go now; my grandmother's going to call me."

Now Maman dials Jude's number, thinking he must want to talk to her. But there is no answer. She explains that this has happened before.

Again the telephone rings, and when Maman answers, she experiences the same frustrating one-sided conversation.

Within minutes there is another ring. This time when Maman says, "Hello," Jude replies. He asks her why she has called. She replies that she didn't call, that he had called her. Both are as dismayed as we are to learn that neither had called the other. The phone simply rang at both houses at the same moment.

Then Maman asks Jude if he had just been talking to Chris. No, he had not! Failing to make sense of the incident, they both break off the connection, only to have a recurrence a few moments later. This time, Maman asks Jude to come over to visit with us. Jude declines, saying he has no transportation.

Not long afterwards, the phone rings again, and this time Jude asks when we are coming over. He claims that Maman had called back and said to get dressed and be ready because we were coming to pick him up.

"Jude," she says, "I didn't say that! Is that really you?"

Yes, he replies, it really is. Incredibly, he had actually heard her voice on the phone saying something she did not say. Just as she had heard his voice earlier saying something he said he had not said....

I desperately want to make sense of this confusion, but the whole incident defies reason. Has some entity drained our recorder batteries only to use the same energy on the telephone? Could it also have reproduced the voices? Or has Jude simply engineered a crafty deception?

Both Maman and Nell seem to read my mind and quickly come to Jude's defense. No, he is not the type of boy to play tricks on his old grandmother. On the contrary, he is quite concerned over what she has been going through. Not to mention the batteries in the tape recorder which Jude could not possibly have touched....

The telephone conversations with Jude continue. After about the dozenth time, with Maman and Jude exchanging confusion over the phone, Nell and I decide to tour the house. *Now* I have chills. The very air seems to be alive and running its icy fingers up and down my spine.

I can scarcely wait to get out of the house, not so much because of the chill, but to give Maman, that poor, dear lady, some peace. For I truly feel that Leonce is behind the telephone calls, purposely making his presence known for our benefit.

As we say our good-byes on the front porch, I can still hear that incessant ringing, ringing, ringing. And I am chilled to the bone.

GLENDA'S GHOST

"It started the minute we built the house. It's not constant but it's frequent. And when it starts, it's very loud."

Glenda (not her real name) is telling me about the activities she attributes to a ghost in her house—"My ghost," she calls it. She is a nurse, perhaps fifty-years-old, and lives in a Cape Cod Colonial that she and her husband designed for their property in New Iberia. She explains that the property was formerly a rice field: "Good ole blackjack soil!" she proclaims, leading me into her living room.

The family owns a processing plant in New Iberia, and they hired workers from the plant to build their home. Later they tried to get the wives of some of these same men to baby-sit for them in the house, but to no avail. The wives had heard too many frightening tales from their husbands.

A realistic person, she was determined to find out what was going on. Why were things moving around? What was the knocking noise? Whose footsteps did she hear when she was alone? And why couldn't she get a baby-sitter?

She says she went down to the plant, sat down with "the whole crowd," and asked them what was in the house. What was going on?

One of them answered, "You've got to be over a pot of gold, or a coffin."

Glenda was mystified. The land had always been cultivated, so she didn't know what might lie buried underneath the house. No one had ever died there—at least not to her knowledge. There were no Civil War battles on the site, no known cemeteries, or anything else out of the ordinary: "Only one thing comes to mind. This is the highest land this side of the bayou, so we've wondered if maybe it was a burial ground for an Indian tribe."

Indians or not, she knows something is in the house, and always has been: "It gets very upset when things are changed. There are sounds like walking, moving things, making noise in general, bumping things around, just knocking."

She leads me into the dining room and points at the furniture: "This furniture...as big as it is, has been moved around several times, the table pushed sideways." But she quickly adds, "There's never any damage. It just gets restless every once in a while and bumps and knocks things around."

This is small comfort for Maggie, one of Glenda's daughters. She refuses to sleep alone in her upstairs room because she's seen mysterious lights there. She's also been awakened a time or two with the distinct impression that someone was breathing on her, or touching her.

Others are equally frightened. For example, her daughter-in-law won't come into the house at all unless someone is with her. Neither will she sit between the kitchen and library doorway, because she always gets the feeling that someone is staring at her.

And has Glenda ever seen anything?

"I have never seen my ghost...but we were having a party outside with a few couples one afternoon. This was before the upstairs was finished. One of the ladies looked up and asked me, 'Who is that man up there in the window?'

"I said I didn't see anyone, but she said, 'Well, look, he's looking right at us.'"

Though she looked, she saw nothing. "But a couple of other people have seen him. I've only heard him."

Heard, indeed. She tells me about the time, only a few days ago, when she was in the kitchen: "I heard 'boomp, boomp, boomp.' I go in the living room and I could have sworn I heard someone walking up the stairs, but I was all alone."

There are other times that he gets so loud she has to turn on the radio to drown him out. "I know this sounds crazy," she says, laughing.

Sometimes he does playful things, like opening the closet doors in the master bedroom in the middle of the night. And since the closet light is activated by the movement of the doors, it would come on at the same moment. Glenda put a stop to that by removing the automatic switch.

After all these years, Glenda still doesn't know who or what is causing the disturbance, though she is beginning to suspect that it is a "gentlemanly old colored man." He may occasionally frighten people, but he's not harmful or evil, and seems to be perfectly happy just walking around the house. "But, oh," she adds, smiling, "he does like to move things around."

STRANGERS IN THE NIGHT

There is a big white building on a lonely stretch of the Evangeline Thruway east of Broussard that once served as a television studio. A petroleum company is housed there now. And perhaps a ghost or two.

Conrad Maxwell should know. A big man in his thirties, he's the station manager for KTDY Radio in Lafayette. But back in 1973, when he was a "switcher" for Channel 15, he sat down for a leisurely chat with one of the resident ghosts, though he didn't realize it at the time.

I visit him at his office, and he prefaces his experiences by telling me what a switcher is: "He's the guy who pushes the buttons to change from one commercial to another, or one program to another. It's like a disc jockey, only for television."

As for the ghosts, Conrad says that lots of things were going on: "The place was just generally kind of spooky and there were stories I just didn't pay much attention to."

But he did pay attention to the lights, especially when they came on by themselves: "Every Sunday morning we'd have a live show called 'Happy Fats.' I'd go out before the show and get things warmed up, put the lights on and the cameras in place. Sometimes in a TV station with a lot of power, a circuit will overload and a light will kick off. But...in this instance the lights *came on!*"

The unusual thing about this incident, explains Conrad, is that the lights had to be operated by a circuit breaker: "It's not just a light switch; it's a lever you have to push over and push back. It was a strange thing!"

Then there was the bright Sunday morning when he encountered a cold spot near the restrooms: "It was about six-thirty on a spring day. I walked into the office area and I was going through the lobby toward the control room...when I came to this area about thirty degrees colder than the rest of the building. It was an area about two-feet wide, and it ran all the way from floor to ceiling.... There were no vents—no drafts to create that kind of environment. It was almost like freezing cold air...almost alive. It gave you kind of an eerie, chilly feeling."

But that was nothing by comparison with his encounter with a non-person. It happened on a Saturday night, when Conrad was working on a long shift. He says it was very noisy in the control room, and he was putting up a video tape when he heard something behind him. He turned to look. Nothing, so he went back to his work. Then he heard the noise again: "I turned around and there was a middle-aged guy standing there with one of those long dust mops...sweeping up. I about jumped out of my skin because I wasn't expecting anybody. I thought I was alone."

Regaining his composure, Conrad went over and introduced himself: "I couldn't tell you what his name was. He was a heavy-set guy pushing a broom around in there. He spoke back to me, shook hands, sat there and shot the breeze with me for fifteen or twenty minutes. I went back to my work and evidently he went on and cleaned up the rest of the place. I never saw him again."

Conrad kept wondering about the janitor. He had never seen anyone there before. So the next time he saw his supervisor, which was two or three days later, he told him, "Look, Tom, next time you put a janitor to work, let me know to expect somebody so I don't jump half way out of my skin."

"But," Tom replied, "we don't have a janitor."

Now Conrad was really perplexed, and, thinking someone was playing jokes on him, took it up with Bill McGoffin, the operations' director.

Bill told him the same thing: "We don't have a janitor."

Conrad says he wasn't the only person to encounter strange things at the old studio. One employee was so frightened after working the night shift that he left abruptly, and wouldn't even come back to the building to pick up his paycheck....

Then there was the case of Sally Bowers, who worked in the building *after* Channel 15 abandoned it in 1975. Sally, an Oklahoman, worked for Oil Well Drilling Company from 1976 to 1985, and it is by sheer good fortune that I manage to interview her.

I go to the building to take a photograph, and walk inside to request permission. The receptionist becomes alert and inquisitive when I tell her my business. So does Jeanette Lewis, the company accountant. It soon becomes clear that they, too, know something of the reputation of the place. And indeed, before long they are relating stories of their own about strange noises and dark shadows. They also tell me about Sally, who had been employed by the former tenants of the building. But it turns out that Sally now lives in Michigan.

Noting my disappointment, the resourceful and thoughtful accountant picks up a phone and dials a number, and within moments, I am speaking with Sally on a direct company line.

Her voice is pleasant and friendly, with a charming Oklahoma accent in spite of the eleven years she lived in Bayou Country. Like many others with whom I have spoken, she is quick to offer a disclaimer: "I don't believe in ghosts," she says, "but...."

Sally says she was on-call one night and had been summoned to the building for an important drafting job. It was midnight when she stood and headed toward the restroom. That's when she noticed someone or something going into the office she had just left: "It was a form all dressed in black...a long flowing cape with an upturned collar. I followed it...but there was no one there."

Whatever it was could not possibly have exited without her seeing it. Yet the office was empty and silent. So she searched the place, looking under desks, behind filing cabinets, and even in the closets. "There was no one there!" she says, her voice taking on an incredulous tone.

I ask her what she thought it was.

"I have no explanation for what happened."

And was she frightened?

"It raised the hair on the back of my neck. It was such an eerie feeling." She also says that since she had to remain there—alone—until 4 a.m., she called answering service just to hear a human voice.

Sally laughs about it now, and mentions that others have dismissed such reports as silly. "But," she adds, "I sure saw that!"

After our phone conversation, Jeanette is kind enough to show me the place where Sally had her close encounter. I wonder aloud if I am the only person who gets goose flesh just standing here.

No, Jeanette assures me, other people have felt it too, including herself. And nowadays none of them will stay in the building after the sun goes down. After all, she tells me, who wants to round a corner in the middle of night and run into a janitor who doesn't belong there, or a shadowy figure dressed in black?

TIME TRAVELER

Local magician, author, and TV talent, Ken Meaux, writes a column for Strange Magazine called "High Strangeness." In a recent edition he reported a time-warp incident which occurred in South Louisiana. He was kind enough to give me permission to retell the story here.

On October 20, 1969, a Lafayette insurance businessman whom I shall call Mr. X was returning to Lafayette after having lunch in Abbeville. An associate was driving the car. The Abbeville Highway stretched barren before their lone vehicle until they noticed an antique car moving slowly ahead.

As they approached it from the rear, Mr. X, who has an avid interest in history and antiques, remarked on the excellent condition of the automobile. He noted the large bright orange 1940 license plate, which is legal only for parade vehicles. The two men were so impressed with the vintage condition of the turtle-back style car that they slowed as they passed to get a better look.

The young lady driver was wearing what appeared to be 1940-style garb, including a hat with a long colored feather and a fur coat. A child standing on the seat next to her was also dressed for winter, with an overcoat and cap. Yet the weather that fall day was pleasant enough for an open window and little more than a sweater.

Mr. X, who was in the passenger seat, decided to compliment the lady on her beautifully-kept car. He got her attention by signaling out of his window, but he was perplexed to see her reaction. She became startled and looked confused. She frantically glanced from him to the automobile in which he rode, and then to her surroundings with nothing less than alarm showing in her face. Clearly she was disoriented and close to tears.

He asked if she was lost and needed help, and motioned for her to pull over to the shoulder. Since her window was closed, he had to repeat this with gestures several times. She finally nodded in agreement and began to drive off to the side of the highway.

Mr. X and his companion drove on around and pulled off to the side in front of her. Then they turned around...and were astonished to note that she was gone, vanished, both the woman *and the antique automobile*. There were no side streets or other places she could have gone or hidden from their sight. She had simply disappeared.

Then a third vehicle approached from the same direction they had come. It stopped, and a very confused driver got out excitedly demanding an explanation for what he had just seen. He said the old car had been pulling over to the side right in front of him. Then, right before his eyes, it disappeared.

This third witness was so distraught over the incident that he insisted on reporting what he had seen to the police. But the other two men questioned the wisdom of such action, pointing out that their sanities would probably be impugned, and eventually converted him to their way of thinking.

Still, the three of them walked the area for an hour, looking in vain for anything that might explain the inexplicable, perhaps a hole in the ground, or a side road, or a water-filled drainage ditch. Finding nothing of the sort, they exchanged names and addresses. They kept in touch for years thereafter, exchanging questions and reassuring one another that they had not imagined the incident.

Does all time coexist? Did the lady and her automobile cross into another dimension, perhaps in some sort of time-warp? It's an intriguing thought with no answers, and, yet, one cannot help but wonder if the newspapers of the 1940's record the disappearance of a woman and her child. Could they still be living? If so, would she recognize a description of the incident? Or does she believe that the perplexing time she became lost was nothing but a confusing dream?

THE HAUNTED RECTORY

Does a long dead priest wander the hallways of a rectory in Abbeville, sometimes knocking on doors and calling out names? Or is it the sound of the wind, and the settling noises of an old building? Father Donald Theriot readily admits that he doesn't have a satisfactory explanation. Neither do the other two priests with whom I spoke.

The rectory stands next to the Church of St. Mary Magdalene. Once a square, graceless structure with a dark interior—the result of long-ago renovations—it has recently been restored to its former glory, with broad galleries, balconies, plenty of sunlight, and the Spanish influence of its original designers.

Father Donald Theriot is the author of these changes. He is also the pastor of St. Mary

Magdalene. I recently had an opportunity to visit with him at the rectory. A friend goes with me, one of Father Theriot's former parishioners, and we are warmly received and taken on a walking tour.

Along the way, Father Theriot, a solidly built, graying man who looks distinguished in his Roman collar and dark priests' garb, points out the ancient stained glass in the pastor's study. He also shows us the water colors by Frank Will on the walls of the parlor, and a large oil painting of Abbe Antoine D. Megret, who founded the town of Abbeville.

An authority on local history, Father Theriot entertains us with stories about the church, the town of Abbeville, and the previous inhabitants of the rectory. Most intriguing are his accounts of the discoveries that were made during the restoration: a wine cellar, the lovely interior archways behind wall paneling, the wooden floors beneath the carpets, the large but empty safe behind a false wall, and the snakes that kept getting into the rectory, disturbing the priests' sleep and creating quite a commotion.

But snakes are not the only creatures that have created a commotion in this beautiful building. Though loathsome and frightening, they can at least be controlled, and indeed, were kept out of the good priests' bedrooms by towels stuffed under the doors. Not so the other intruders, the ones I was anxious to hear about from Father Theriot.

I had heard ghost stories about this place for months, in one instance from a priest who was a former resident. I'll call him Father Octavio since he wishes to remain anonymous. He told me about the experiences of an elderly priest who also lived there at the time, and whose bedroom was in a parlor where yet another priest had previously died. This elderly priest would frequently be awakened during the night by loud knocks at his door. Each time he answered, however, there would be nothing on the other side but an empty hallway.

Could he have been just dreaming about the knocks at the door?

"No," Father Octavio assured me. The priest was "not given to hallucinations."

On another occasion, Father Octavio arrived home late one night to find the old priest wandering the corridor in his pajamas. A puzzled look was on his face. When asked what he was doing, he explained that he had heard someone walking in the hallway and had gotten up to investigate, but found nothing. "I know he wouldn't have fabricated any of this," Father Octavio added.

Then there was the time the cook heard someone calling out her name in the middle of the day although she was alone; and the night the pastor heard footsteps on the stairway, though no one was there at that hour; and the time that Father Octavio himself heard "spooky" noises in the kitchen: "But it was a windy night and I attribute it to the wind," he said, smiling. Father Octavio closed our interview by saying that most of the noises were attributed, in jest, to the priest who had died there.

The priest who died there was Father Edmund Daull, a well-loved, colorful man from a small town in France. Father Theriot shows me his portrait in the parish office and mentions that he died of a cardiac arrest in 1949. From the portrait I judge he must have been in his mid-forties. It seems that when he came over from France he brought a dozen valuable watercolors with him. Some of them have since disappeared, and I cannot help but wonder if Father Daull might still be walking the halls and knocking on doors to inquire about his precious watercolors—or to tell someone where they can be found.

Father Theriot has also heard these noises. Speaking in a calm, comforting voice, he points to a blank wall during our tour and says that it was once the location of a bathroom door: "One morning about five I was in the bathroom shaving and there was the loudest knock on the door. My name was called, and I was sure it was Father LeBlanc [who also lived there]. I went to the door and looked up and down the hall. No one."

A slow smile comes over his face as he relates the story, and says it was kind of interesting because whoever it was had called him by his first name, "and the ghost and I are not on intimate terms."

We descend the wooden stairway where so many mysterious footsteps have been heard, and continue our conversation in an airy, sitting room next to the kitchen. And again Father Theriot talks about the footsteps: "I was in the living room—this was before the house was finished—and heard the sound of footsteps up above me in the hall...back and forth, back and forth. Oftentimes a priest will read his breviary while walking, so I figured Father Moreau was back from his visit to Eunice."

After a while, Father Theriot decided to go to the church and turn on the air conditioning for evening services: "And as I went out the back door,

Father Moreau came around the church square returning from Eunice. So I was the only one in the house when I heard the footsteps [which] went on for a good ten minutes—and loud. Of course, I realize, as you do, that old houses make noise. But what I heard upstairs were definitely footsteps, so...."

I ask Father Theriot what he thinks could be behind the disturbances. His answer is tinged with a smile and occasional laughter: "I don't know if he's trying to tell us something. I think maybe he was displeased with what was done with the rectory all those years ago...so dark and dreary. Maybe the ghost was more comfortable with the dark existence too. Maybe now that there's light, it moved on to some other place. Ever since the restoration was completed we don't have the occurrences."

After my interview with Father Theriot, I decide to call Father Ronald Groth, now of Kinder, who lived at the rectory from 1973 to 1976. Over the telephone I ask him if he had ever had any encounters with the resident ghost. His answer is quick and enthusiastic: "Yes, I did!"

It seems that about six months after Father Groth moved in, he also began hearing noises: "I was alone one night on the second floor. The old stairs creaked below me. I heard someone walking. No one came up, and I saw no one down the long hall."

He says it started up again, this time near the doorway: "The noises were very real. I grabbed a tennis racquet with a big wooden brace and walked to the door.... I threw it open. Not a soul there!"

Father Groth also tells me about another priest who not only heard the walking but actually saw footprints form in the carpet, like an invisible presence walking down the long corridor.

After discussing that for a while, I ask him about the Church's position on the subject of ghosts.

"The Church has long recognized the existence of poltergeists," he said.

And how does he personally feel?

"Well," he answers, chuckling, "I'm not one to believe in ghosts, "but I had an experience [the night of the footsteps]."

I had previously put the same questions to the other priests. Father Octavio's answer: "Theologically, I have trouble with it because at death there is immediate judgment. Either one is saved or not. Where the soul goes is determined by the judgment of God."

And Father Theriot's: "I don't think it's against our religion to believe in ghosts. There are people who have appeared—who have come back. We believe in the supernatural. Personally, I'm not a believer in ghosts, but I really don't know what to think."

So the mystery remains. What was in the rectory and what did it want? I have no idea, but I often think of Father Theriot's words: "I think people could come back to plead for prayers and assistance, but as far as doing evil, no. There's a lot we don't understand. Let's face it."

THEOLOGICALLY SPEAKING

My pastor, Father Robie Robichaux of Sacred Heart Catholic Church in Broussard, was kind enough to share his thoughts with me on the subject of ghosts. Based on his considerable education in theology, he explained the Church's teachings. He also expressed his personal beliefs.

From strictly a theological point of view, the Church has been very good about where she stands on that kind of a thing. And from a theological point of view we believe that once a person has died, they have died. There is no coming back, so to speak, in the form of a ghost.
    Certainly we have instances of apparitions. For instance, saints, our Blessed Mother, even our Lord Himself. Whether or not these are really and truly actual—from the point of view that it has the Church's stamp on it saying that these apparitions actually occurred—no, it doesn't; not even at the major reported apparitions of Fatima and Lourdes; these do not have official Church stamp of approval because they can't be proven. All the Church has said is that if anything did happen it doesn't go contrary to faith or morals. So from that point of view, there is always the possibility of an apparition.
    The Church is very clear about the thing of ghosts and whatnot as being non-existent, as going contrary to our belief in what happens to us at death and after death. Based on Church teaching over the past 2000 years, there's been no such thing

as a disembodied spirit—that it's mislocated somewhere.

After death, a person's soul, prior to being united with the body at the last judgment, participates in the life of Heaven to one degree or another, or the absence of that life in condemnation. You have the question of Purgatory where that comes in. In a sense Purgatory is a participation in the life of Heaven because that is the ultimate end of the soul.

The point that I'm trying to make here is this: since the breath of life was breathed into a soul by God Himself, the soul participates in God's life to one degree or another. It would not, therefore—according to Church teaching—be found wandering around looking for a place to go.

Purgatory is a state of being, a state of purification. The soul would have to know what it is missing, so therefore the soul would have to have encountered the presence of God in one way or another. Whether or not this state takes place on earth or after death as a means of God exercising His mercy and His compassion certainly can take place. It's a state of being; it's not a place.

Of course we're dealing with spiritual realities and talking about them in physical terms. There's no such thing as *time* with God. Eternity is timelessness.

Purgatory is not a situation whereby a soul is wandering about aimlessly. Purgatory is controlled by God. God is not known to let go of His possessions like that. All of this is strictly from a theological point of view.

Personally, I do not believe in ghosts. I am

always amused by ghost stories; I love ghost stories. I'm fascinated by them. I do admit that there are certain phenomena that perhaps we cannot explain. And I certainly leave open the possibility or the idea...whether or not you attribute it to a ghost I guess depends on your particular bias.

I do not look down upon or criticize or condemn anyone who may believe in ghosts. They may have good reason, for all I know.

I accept the fact that certain phenomena can happen that we cannot readily explain in black and white terms.

I think all of this—theories and postulations—is good in a sense because we recognize that we're more than just flesh and bones. That there is a spiritual side to us. If we accept that, then we also have to accept that there is another dimension to us other than that which is perceived by the senses, that which is just corporeal, and governed by things which are corporeal, like time. So, from that point of view, it's good.

How we come to understand how that side of ourselves manifests itself, well, I'm not too sure we'll ever come to understand it because it's so foreign to our human experiences of senses. And I'm not too sure we'd know how to handle it. Maybe that's why God saved the spiritual side for Heaven.

But it's fascinating. I've always enjoyed thinking about ghosts and the spiritual side.

There's evidence of at least a thinking about it at the time of Christ and even before that. But this belief in ghosts, to my way of thinking, seemed to intensify during the Middle Ages, the Dark Ages. There was a tremendous interest in our spiritual side—trying to explain God's mercy and justice. A lot of our notions about ghosts are medieval.

I do believe that we have the ability to be psychic, to discern, predict or see more clearly. It is legitimate that there is ESP, having to do with a person's makeup, based on certain "givens."

The thing that we always want to be very careful about is that we don't want to limit God as to what He can do and who He can use. The other side of that coin is that not everything that everybody does and claims to be done by God through them is actually His work.

INDEX

Abbeville, 85, 132, 135-36
Acadiana, 29
Accidents, tragic, 7
Advertiser, Daily, 107
Aleman, Pete, 85
Allgood, John, 69-70
Amelie, 102, 109
Apparitions, 30, 34-35, 37, 56, 58, 70, 72-73, 77, 80-82, 93-94, 100, 107, 109, 125, 128-30, 141
Babineaux, Allen, 97, 101
Babineaux, Anne, 97-101
Babineaux, Frank, 100
Babineaux, Jami, 99
Babineaux, Jena, 99
Babineaux, Joni, 100
Banks, Gen. Nathaniel, 32, 83
Barbara, 119-20
Barry, 25-28
Baton Rouge, 84
Battle Bayou Bourbeux, 1, 5-7, 83
Bayless family, 60, 63, 65
Betty, 44
Bidstrup, Dr. Richard, 69-70
Big Foot, 51
Billeaud, Andy, 21-23
Billeaud, Beau, 19-21
Billeaud, Mike, 18-24
Billeaud, Sally, 19
Blood-stained floors, 30, 76
Bond, Priscilla, 85
Bourbeux Bayou, 1, 5-7, 83
Bowers, Sally, 129-30
Brasseaux, Carl, 85
Broussard, 28, 93, 127
Butcher Switch, 25
Buzzard's Prairie, 75
Cajuns, 63, 77, 105-06
Canadian, 115
Carencro Bayou, 76
Carencro, 29
Carriere, Gerard, 32
Carrington house, 33, 35
Carson, Johnny, 107
Centerville, 43
Chicago Mercantile Battery, 79
Civil War, 1, 5-6, 30-32, 43, 64, 69, 75-85, 92, 120, 124
Cold spots, 128
Comeaux, Julie, 93-96
Comeaux, Oneziphore, 103
Confederates, 83-84
Connie, 52-55
Cottage, the, 61, 64
Coussan, Stephen, 104

Creation Studios, 71
Crowley, 51
Daull, Father Edmund, 137-38
Daylight, 64
Dead Man's Curve, 87, 90
Delahoussaye Canal, 11
Delcambre, 65
Dianne, 25-28
Dupuy's Island, 60
Edmonds, Alex, 80
Edmonds, Christopher, 78, 85
Edmonds, David, 6, 75-85
Edmonds, Julie, 79-83
Edmonds, Lucinda, 75-85
Elliott, 19
Eunice, 138-39
Extra-sensory perception, 88
Fatima, 141
Feu Follet, 50
Fletcher, Cherie, 111
Fletcher, Glen, 113-14
Fletcher, Mike, 111-14
Franklin, 43, 111
Fulbright professor, 77
Garden City, 43
Glenda, 124-26
Grand Coteau, 5, 85-86, 87
Grand Marais, 11
Grand Prairie, 28, 115
Groth, Father Ronald, 139-40
Gue, Jeremiah, 83-85
Guidry, Constance, 75, 81-83
Guilbeau, Brandon, 87-92
Guilbeau, Dixie, 87-92
Guilbeau, Tim, 87-88
Gulf of Mexico, 11
Harmonic Progression, 108
Harris, Addie, 43-44, 48
Hospitals, Civil War, 30, 69, 79
House of History, 28
Houston, 25
Howard, Mr., 11, 15
Hudson River, 101
Hunter, James, 81
Hutslar, Kent, 71-74
Iberia Parish, 8, 97
Ile Carencro, 75-76, 78, 83
Indiana, 60th Inf., 81
Iowa, 24th Inf., 83
Iowa, 84
Jefferson Island Cafe, 66-67
Jefferson Island, 59-68
Jefferson house, 59, 61
Jefferson, Joseph, 59-60, 68

Jude, 120-23
KTDY Radio, 127
Kathy, 20-21
La. State Un., 84-85
Lafayette, 18, 25, 56, 95, 127
Lafitte, Jean, 11, 64
Lagniappe Cafe, 71-72
Lake Charles, 107, 119
Landry, Christy, 15
Landry, Dana, 15
Landry, Jackie, 8-17
Landry, Jeremi, 14
Landry, Joyce, 8-17, 66-67
LeBlanc, Father, 138
LeBourgeois building, 71-74
Leger, Larry, 5-7
Leonce, 119-20, 123
Lewis, Jeanette, 129-31
Live Oak Gardens, 60-61
Louella, 103
Louisiana, Miss, 30
Lourdes Hospital, 25
Lourdes, miracle at, 141
Madonna, 117
Maggie, 125
Mamalakis, Mario, 107
Maman, 115-23
Marland, William, 6
Marshmallow, 90-92
Martin, Carrol, 71
Martin, Isaac, 71
Massachusetts soldiers, 5-6
Maxwell, Conrad, 127-29
Mayan calendar, 108
McGoffin, Bill, 129
Meaux, Ken, 132
Medal of Honor, 6
Megret, Abbe Antoine, 136
Melancon, Bobbie, 29
Metairie, 19
Mexico, 77
Miller's Island, 60
Mississippi, 83
Missy, 36-41
Montgomery, Russell, 2, 6-7
Morain, Gerry, 33-35
Morbihan, 97
Moreau, Father, 138-39
Moseley, Charlie, 106-07, 109
Moseley, Mary, 105
Moseley, Matthew, 104, 110
Moseley, Peggy, 102-110
Murders, 2
Nell, 115, 120-23
New Iberia, 52, 54, 59, 71, 73, 97, 100, 124
Nicholson, Mildred, 28-33
Nims' Battery, 6
Nova Scotia, 119
Octavio, Father, 136-37, 140
Ohio, 17th Battery, 79
Oil Well Drilling Co., 129
Oklahoma, 129-30
Olivier, Suzanne, 107

Opelousas, 2, 29, 69, 76
Oppenheimer, Paul, 2, 5
Orange Island, 60
Patout, Roy, 62-63
Patricia, 104
Patsy's Cafe, 33
Peigneur Lake, 60, 67-68
Pennsylvania, 29
Pirates, 9-11, 16, 64
Poiret Place, 69-70
Poltergeist activity, 26-27, 87-88
Prissy, Miss, 54-55
Purgatory, 142
Reader's Digest, 101
Richard, Mike, 61, 64
Robichaux, Father Robie, 141-44
Rosie, 29
Salt Dome, 60
Sarah Plantation, 97-98
Sarah's curse, 101
Shirlene, 66-67
Simonette Lake, 60
Southern Baptist, 105
Spanish Trail Nursery, 47
St. Landry Parish, 1, 6, 69
St. Martinville, 36
St. Mary Magdalene, 135
Stagecoach road, 76
Stagg Records, 72
Steve, 23-24
Strange Magazine, 132
Sturgis, David, 3-4
Sturgis, Kathy, 3-4, 7
Sunset, 1, 75
Susie Plantation, 42-43, 45
Texaco, 67
Texas soldiers, 1, 6
T-Frere's B&B, 102
Theriot, Bob, 65
Theriot, Father Donald, 135-40
Time travel 132-34
Tom, 129
Traiteurs, 32, 64, 96
Treasure, buried, 64, 91-92
Un. of Southwestern La., 56, 77, 82, 87
Van Winkle, Rip, 59
Vermilion Bay, 11
Vermilionville, 76
Voodoo Land, 64
Wadsworth, Jane, 65
Washington, 28-28, 33, 115
Washington, D.C., 79
Wicks, Lydia, 45
Wicks, Mary Lee, 42-46
Will, Frank, 136
Ziegler, Dana, 50
Ziegler, Jeannie, 47-51
Ziegler, Manuel, 48, 51
Ziegler, Robert, 49-50
Ziegler, Teeny, 48-51
Ziegler, Trina, 48

Christine Word is a freelance writer and lecturer on various topics. For information about her presentations, write her at
106 Brigante Place
Lafayette, LA 70508